THE WRITING LIFE OF
JAMES D. WATSON

THE WRITING LIFE OF JAMES D. WATSON

ERROL C. FRIEDBERG

University of Texas Southwestern Medical Center
Dallas, Texas

We are most grateful for major support from
The Lehrman Institute for the preparation of this book

COLD SPRING HARBOR LABORATORY PRESS
COLD SPRING HARBOR, NEW YORK

THE WRITING LIFE OF JAMES D. WATSON

© 2005 by Cold Spring Harbor Laboratory Press, Cold Spring Harbor, New York
Printed in the United States of America

Publisher	John Inglis
Editorial Development Manager	Jan Argentine
Developmental Editors	Jody Tressider, Judy Cuddihy, Elizabeth Powers
Project Coordinators	Joan Ebert, Mary Cozza, Maryliz Dickerson
Image Coordinator	Elizabeth Powers
Permissions Coordinator	Maria Falasca
Production Editor	Kathleen Bubbeo
Desktop Editor	Susan Schaefer
Production Manager and	
Interior Designer	Denise Weiss
Cover Designer	Ed Atkeson
Director of Cold Spring Harbor	
Laboratory Libraries and Archives	Ludmila Pollock

Front cover photograph: Jim Watson in his office at Harvard University in the late 1960s.

Library of Congress Cataloging-in-Publication Data

Friedberg, Errol C.
  The writing life of James D. Watson / Errol C. Friedberg.
      p. cm.
  ISBN 0-87969-700-8 (hardcover : alk. paper)
  1. Watson, James D., 1928- 2. Molecular biology--Authorship. 3.
Technical writing. 4. Medical writing. I. Title.

  QH506.F746 2004
  572.8--dc22
                        2004015640

10 9 8 7 6 5 4 3 2 1

All Cold Spring Harbor Laboratory Press publications may be ordered directly from Cold Spring Harbor Laboratory Press, 500 Sunnyside Blvd., Woodbury, N.Y. 11797-2924. Phone: 1-800-843-4388 in Continental U.S. and Canada. All other locations: 516-422-4100. FAX: 516-422-4097. E-mail: cshpress@cshl.org. For a complete catalog of all Cold Spring Harbor Laboratory Press publications, visit our World Wide Web Site http://www.cshlpress.com/

For Rhonda

CONTENTS

PREFACE

JAMES WATSON IS FAMOUS FOR DEDUCING, with the late Francis Crick, the structure of DNA, possibly the 20th century's most significant discovery in biology. For this accomplishment, Watson, Crick, and their colleague and competitor Maurice Wilkins received the Nobel Prize in 1962. Yet, when asked what he considers his greatest achievement, Watson's response is unhesitating: It is, he has said firmly, "my writing."

His controversial account of the discovery, *The Double Helix*, has become a classic. But Watson has also produced several textbooks, all commercially successful and at least two of them credited with changing the landscape of biology education, a second memoir that is a sequel to *The Double Helix*, a recent and outstanding book to accompany a television series on genetics, and a prodigious number of essays written for a variety of publications. And there are other works in progress.

This output, over more than 40 years, was accomplished while Watson was fully engaged in the life of a scientist and academic administrator, first as a research and teaching professor at Harvard, then, successively, as Director, President, and Chancellor of the Cold Spring Harbor Laboratory. In addition, he was the first Director of the National Center for Human Genome Research at the National Institutes of Health in Bethesda, Maryland.

Watson's unrivaled record in scientific leadership and public service has been warmly and widely recognized with honors that include innumerable degrees, the Presidential Medal of Freedom (1977), and an honorary Knighthood from the United Kingdom (2002) for services to Anglo-American relations. By comparison, the aspect of himself he points to most proudly, his work as a writer, has received little attention.

In these pages, I do not attempt to deconstruct Watson's literary style and influences or to probe his beliefs and motivations. I do hope to illuminate the remarkable and innovative nature of Jim Watson's written work. He has made strenuous efforts to reach two kinds of audience. The larger group consists of people intrigued by but not trained in science who know Watson only as the discoverer, then chronicler, of the double helix. The second is the community of scientists, particularly those in training, who are familiar with the broad range of Watson's research but unaware, perhaps, of how much more he has done for their education and their profession. Both audiences matter deeply to Watson and, in what follows, his work for each is discussed separately.

ERROL FRIEDBERG
August 2004

ACKNOWLEDGMENTS

THIS BOOK IS BASED ON RESEARCH of original documents from the James D. Watson Special Collection, housed at Cold Spring Harbor Laboratory. In 2000, the Lehrman Institute made a generous grant to Cold Spring Harbor Laboratory to assist the development of the Watson Collection in the Laboratory Archives, under the leadership of Ludmila Pollock, Director of Libraries and Archives. The initiation of this book was one of several projects made possible by the Lehrman funds.

The James D. Watson Special Collection includes an extensive collection of scientific and personal correspondence, photographs from 1928 to the present, teaching notes, clippings, videos, manuscripts, scientific reprints, speeches, and memorabilia—a comprehensive documentation of 60 years' work at the highest levels in science. Unique to the Collection are Watson's own laboratory notebooks from graduate school at Indiana University through his tenure as a Biology Professor at Harvard University, as well as correspondence with other prominent scientists, discussing experiments and research ideas. The teaching files Watson created during his Harvard years detail the teaching methodology and practice that, as discussed in this book, were the essential underpinnings of his pioneering textbook *Molecular Biology of the Gene*. Course syllabi, exams, laboratory applicants, lectures, correspondence, and Watson's handwritten comments on exams, class rosters, and grade sheets document his connection with subsequent generations of molecular biologists, many of whom have become important historical figures in their own right. Much of Watson's letters, manuscripts, and other material related to his eight published books can be found in the Collection.

I am most grateful to Mila Pollock for her support for this book and I thank her and the accommodating and charming staff of the Archives, particularly Clare Bunce, Teresa Kruger, and Cara Brick, for their dedication and patience in helping me sift through masses of archival material, acquiring documents from other sources, and providing transcription of taped interviews.

Jim Watson once described John Inglis, Executive Director of Cold Spring Harbor Laboratory Press, as "an author's publisher." He is indeed. John was a much valued and profoundly honest guide and critic and a source of enormous encouragement throughout the writing of this book. He provided the life raft when drowning seemed imminent, and forced me to withstand waters I sometimes thought too deep. Liz Powers, Jody Tressider, and Judy Cuddihy provided indispensable editorial guidance. Liz Powers provided sharp editorial focus when much was needed. This is in many ways as much her book as it is mine, though I exonerate her from any errors and shortcomings that remain. Kathy Bubbeo was also enormously helpful in bringing the manuscript to completion.

Thanks to Jan Witkowski, Executive Director of the Banbury Center, and Bruce Stillman, Director (now President and CEO) of the Cold Spring Harbor Laboratory, for their hospitality in facilitating a memorable period of writing in residence and for their general support and friendship. I am indebted to Bruce Alberts, George Andreou, Andrew Berry, Libby Borden, Walter Gratzer, John Inglis, David Kurtz, Neil Patterson, Heather Raff, Martin Raff, Keith Roberts, Michael Rodgers, John Tooze, Jim Watson, Jan Witkowski, and Norton Zinder for interviews and discussions. I also thank Libby Borden,

Walter Gratzer, Neil Patterson, Heather Raff, and Michael Rodgers for providing illustrative materials.

Particular thanks to my wife Rhonda, my constant companion and cheerleader, who read countless drafts—and never failed to improve them—and to my sister Pearl Benater (a demanding former English teacher) who diligently addressed my grammatical errors. Thanks also to Bryn Bridges, Angela Ceplis, Pila Estess, Tomas Lindahl, Alex Gann, Trefor Jenkins, Nitin Karandikar, Martin Kessel, Nancy Schneider, Roger Schultz, Keith Wharton, Ruth Womack, Rick Wood, and Jan Witkowski who read the manuscript in various stages of preparation and offered numerous helpful comments, suggestions, and criticisms. Angela Ceplis, Jeanine Moore, Meredith Thomas, and Theresa West copied and collated multiple drafts, transcribed taped interviews, maintained masses of files, fed me gallons of coffee, and generally kept me in touch with my professional life as a scientist and university administrator through which I still earn my living.

Finally, and most particularly, I thank Jim Watson for his unflagging accessibility, and for his complete lack of interference in the execution of this labor. Jim never once asked to see any part of the manuscript prior to publication and, when invited to do so, unhesitatingly declined.

FOREWORD

WHEN ERROL FRIEDBERG ASKED ME to write a foreword to this book, I was surprised to hear that it was not about the persona and scientific work of Jim Watson but about his writing. Notice not his *writings*, though these are included in detail (and letting Jim speak for himself is the best way of understanding his massive contribution to 20th century biology). The book is about Jim as an author. His friends know that Jim has literary as well as scientific ambitions.

Unlike our colleagues in the humanities, scientists pay little heed to the form and style of what they read and are intent on extracting content. My generation was forced by the editors and customs of scientific journals to write a scholastic form of English, the origin of which is Teutonic-Latin rather than Anglo-Saxon. The use of the pronouns "I" and "we" was strictly forbidden; instead the cumbersome phrase "the present author (or authors)" was required. Blunt and plain statements were denied: We could not say that other scientists were wrong or that they talked complete rubbish. Rather we had to say that their interpretations of the data were incomplete and this had led them to erroneous conclusions. Anglo-Saxon English was frowned upon. I was asked by an editor to change the word "about" in the phrase "about five days" to "approximately" on the grounds that this was more accurate. I once traced the evolution of the Anglo-Saxon word "blend" to the Teuton-Latin "blendorize" in the pages of *Journal of Biological Chemistry*. A piece of apparatus called a Waring Blendor had been invented and both the action and the process had undergone technical transformation. I believe I did once hear the next stage of "blendoriza-tionize" in a seminar, but never saw it in print.

This imposition of formulaic technical jargon made most scientific writing extremely dull and turgid. As a student, I discovered the writings of the Oxford philosopher R.G. Collingwood and became a great admirer of his prose. He wrote plain English using mostly words of one syllable. He could give you a clear view of his thoughts in reams of such words. It is quite hard to do this in science, with its many new terms and fused words, but it is an end we should all aim at. (There! I have done it—an editor would have asked me to improve it by saying "R.G. Collingwood's presentation of his philosophical . . . .")

I have several friends who are professional literary critics and I asked their advice before embarking on writing the foreword to this book of Errol Friedberg's. Does one look at form and style these days? No, they assured me, that is old hat and very academic. What about the history of ideas? I ask. That is a little more interesting, but hard work, since putting a writer in his context in both time and space requires not only a knowledge of his works but of everybody else both past and present, and, if we are to believe some critics, future as well. Does Friedberg discuss any works of fiction? they inquire. Well, one book—*The Double Helix*—might be considered so. Ah, they say, so you might comment on whether or not it has been properly deconstructed and if Friedberg has revealed his position in relation to the events and characters depicted by the book; indeed you might deconstruct yourself in a foreword, so that reviewers can include you as well as Friedberg and Watson.

You will find none of that here. This book is an account of Jim as writer, an account of his writing and its influence. It includes not only his books but other works such as his annual reports as head of Cold Spring Harbor Laboratory, which offer commentaries not only on science but also on the impact of science on the world outside. Jim's book

The Double Helix is a famous (to some, infamous) account of the discovery of the double helical structure of DNA. It is an autobiography intertwined with a history and whatever one lacks is compensated by the other. I believe that Jim's most important contribution is his book *Molecular Biology of the Gene.* This brought the new science to the attention of many students and explained the fusion of genetics and biochemistry to a generation of eager readers. It introduced a new style of scientific exposition, more Anglo-Saxon than Teutonic-Latin, and very different from the textbooks of biochemistry that my generation was made to read. Indeed, it is my belief that Jim invented a style that could be called the "Massachusetts Declarative" and became the hallmark of the journal *Cell* and many of today's publications.

Of course, I am bound to say that you should read this book. But do not be like many people I know who read only the reviews of books and not the books themselves. Enjoy Errol Friedberg's work as a commentary and guide, but if you have not already done so, go and read the original Watson.

SYDNEY BRENNER

INTRODUCTION

A LIFE OF WRITING

"I was born into a family with three paramount values. One was the importance of books and the belief that knowledge would liberate mankind from superstition." JDW, *A PASSION FOR DNA*, P. 3.

James (Jim) Watson was born into a family that "believed in books"[1] and their house was filled with hundreds of them. Even though the Great Depression of the 1930s brought financial strain to the family, books were always an essential in the Watson home. The books came from the Book of the Month Club, the used bookshops in Chicago's Loop and Hyde Park, and the public library on 73rd Street, to which Jim and his father walked every Friday evening to stock up for the coming week. Although Jim's father favored philosophy, he also kept books on science and it was these that Jim pored over.

Jim's father, James D. Watson, Sr., was a socialist-leaning Democrat[2] and self-educated intellectual who spent his early career at a Chicago business correspondence school. He was a realist who disdained ideas such as astrology and religion that went beyond the laws of science. Watson's mother, Margaret Jean, attended the University of Chicago for two years during the 1920s and then worked at the same business correspondence school her husband attended.

Jim learned from his father to think critically about what he read. In the Watson home *The New Republic* and *The Nation* were the pre-

Jim Watson, portrait at age 10, 1938. (Courtesy of the James D. Watson Collection, Cold Spring Harbor Laboratory Archives.) Watson was an early avid reader. When he was 10, he recalls, he stayed up nights reading the World Almanac.

ferred news magazines, and *The Saturday Evening Post* was "the week-ly magazine that I had been brought up to despise."[3]

Watson's reading taste was eclectic and strongly influenced by his innate curiosity and preference for explanations over descriptions.

Jim Watson, age 11, with his father, James, and his sister, Elizabeth, 1939. (Courtesy of the James D. Watson Collection, Cold Spring Harbor Laboratory Archives.) Watson's father introduced him to literature and the public libraries, as well as to his lifelong interest in bird-watching.

Nonetheless, novels were important to him. Watson himself has commented: "When I think of the young people I grew up with or knew at college I can't think of anyone whom I wanted to really imitate or emulate in any way. The characters in novels were much more real to me than my friends."[4] Novels such as John Dos Passos's *USA* trilogy and James Farrell's Chicago-based *Studs Lonigan* taught Watson, he thought, more about America than he would learn from his daily life.[5] He also read Christopher Isherwood, especially *Mr. Norris Changes Trains*, a now "largely forgotten, marvelously perceptive description of slightly seedy people,"[6] and everything by Graham Greene, including *The End of the Affair* and *The Heart of the Matter*, which made a particularly strong impression on the young Jim Watson. Reading also deepened Jim's interest in biology, especially the heroic scientific fig-

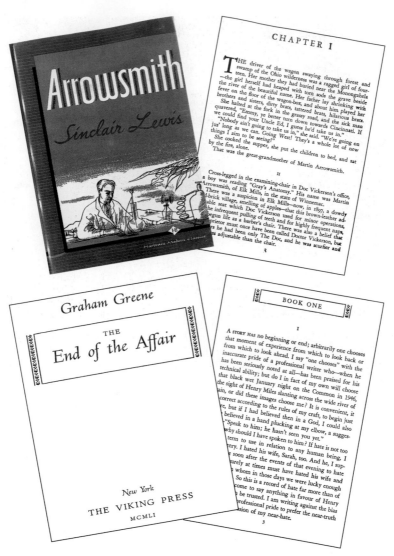

Two of the many books that influenced the young Watson: *Arrowsmith* by Sinclair Lewis and *The End of the Affair* by Graham Greene. Watson has said that the characters in novels were more real to him than his friends. (Back cover and page 1 from *Arrowsmith*, ©1925 by Harcourt, Inc. and renewed 1953 by Michael Lewis, reprinted, by permission of Harcourt, Inc. From *The End of the Affair* by Graham Greene, ©1951, renewed ©1979 by Graham Greene. Used by permission of Viking Penguin, a division of Penguin Group (USA) Inc.)

Franklin D. Roosevelt giving a "fireside chat," April 28, 1935, broadcast from Washington, D.C. (Courtesy of the FDR Library.) On that date he spoke on the Works Relief Program. Watson enjoyed listening to great speakers such as FDR and Winston Churchill, and learned from them the value of well-crafted language.

ures portrayed in Sinclair Lewis's classic *Arrowsmith* and the widely influential *Microbe Hunters* by Paul de Kruif.

Radio also had a powerful influence in the Watson household. During his early years, Jim spent evenings listening to such masters of rhetoric as Franklin D. Roosevelt, Winston Churchill, and the great CBS correspondent Edward R. Murrow—broadcasts that heightened Watson's appreciation for the polished phrase and the well-crafted one-liner.

". . . if the gene is the essence of life, I want to know more about it." JDW, *A PASSION FOR DNA*, P. 123

Jim Watson enjoyed grammar school, and his reading comprehension scores placed him at the top of his class. He entered the University of Chicago at the age of 15 to study zoology, a choice much

Watson, age 18, near his home in Chicago, Illinois, 1946. By age 18 he had graduated from The University of Chicago and had been admitted as a graduate student at Indiana University. (Courtesy of the James D. Watson Collection, Cold Spring Harbor Laboratory Archives.)

influenced by bird-watching, the long-standing interest he shared with his father. The progressive University President Robert M. Hutchins had opened the University to especially promising students, even if they had completed only two years of high school, with an innovative program that offered an unusually broad introduction to Western civilization, "starting with Plato and going through Darwin, Marx, and Freud."[7] Watson went often to the main reading room of Harper Library to research original papers and documents and became a discriminating reader with an appreciation for good writing. He was particularly influenced by *Main Currents in American Thought* by the University of Washington historian, Vernon Parrington, a work that favored coming to grips with economic and religious determinism. This period also cultivated Watson's interest in the history of science.

During his third year, in 1946, the 17-year-old Watson encountered a slim but profoundly influential publication—*What is Life? The Physical Aspect of the Living Cell*[8]—by the famous theoretical physicist Erwin Schrödinger. This book, which was strongly influenced by the

Watson with his family bird-watching on the East Coast, possibly in Maine, 1950. Bird-watching was one of his early interests, shared with his father. *Left to right:* Watson's father, mother, uncle, and sister. Watson is on *far right.* (Courtesy of the James D. Watson Collection, Cold Spring Harbor Laboratory Archives.)

physicist-turned-biologist Max Delbrück (later an important mentor to Watson), suggested that genes, the fundamental units of life, must exist in some sort of distinct physical state that embodied a code. The impact of *What is Life?* on Watson was dramatic:

> *In that little gem, Schrödinger said the essence of life was the gene. Up until then, I was interested in birds. But then I thought, well, if the gene is the essence of life, I want to know more about it. And that was fateful because, otherwise, I would have spent my life studying birds and no one would have heard of me.*[9]

By reading Schrödinger, Watson had his first encounter with the idea that there must be a code of some sort that allowed molecules in cells to carry information.[10] "By the term's end, I had made the decision to have the gene as my life's principal objective."[11]

What is Life? also had a profound influence on other scientists of that era. Francis Crick read the book in 1946 and, according to Watson, it was "a major factor in his [Crick's] leaving physics and developing an interest in biology . . . ."[12] Horace Judson, the historian of the rise of molecular biology, noted:

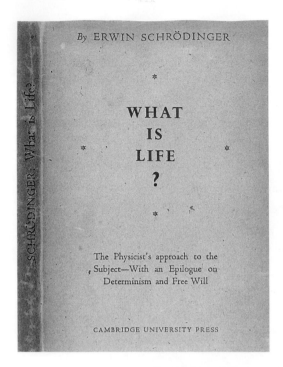

What is Life? by Erwin Schrödinger. (©1945, Cambridge University Press, Cambridge, United Kingdom. Reprinted with the permission of Cambridge University Press.) Watson read this book while he was in college and it profoundly influenced the direction of his scientific career. He has said it "turned him on to the gene."

Everybody read Schrödinger. The fascination of the book lay in the clarity with which Schrödinger approached the gene not as an algebraic unit but as a physical substance that had to be almost perfectly stable and yet express immense variety.[13]

Because of the questions posed by Schrödinger and the nature of the problem of identifying and describing the gene itself, the early development of molecular biology relied greatly on scientists who brought insights from physics to biology—Max Delbrück, Salvador Luria, Leo Szilard, George Gamow, Sir Lawrence Bragg, Francis Crick, Max Perutz, John Kendrew, Maurice Wilkins, Desmond Bernal, and Linus Pauling being the best known of these scientists.

". . . [my] memories of my Ph.D. thesis research are now very limited." JDW to ECF, *Correcting the Blueprint*, p. 23

Jim Watson graduated from the University of Chicago in 1947. The California Institute of Technology (Caltech) was his first choice for graduate school, and he also applied to the Biology Department at Harvard. But Watson's advisor persuaded him to apply also to Indiana University at Bloomington because of its advanced state of genetics, represented by the *Drosophila* geneticist and recent Nobel Laureate Hermann J. Muller, and by several outstanding younger geneticists, Tracy Sonneborn and Salvador Luria among them. Indiana accepted Watson first. Caltech wrote him a letter of rejection that hurt but did not surprise him, and he declined acceptance at Harvard because, in addition to no offer of financial support, "there was no one on the Harvard faculty so up on the gene that I could seriously be tempted to go there."[14]

Watson entered Indiana University in September 1947. His letters to his parents were frequent and chatty, reporting academic progress, occasionally mentioning his love for classical music, especially opera, and describing movies he had seen. His letters also reveal his growing

Watson at Indiana University. He obtained his Ph.D. from the University under Salvador Luria. (Courtesy of the James D. Watson Collection, Cold Spring Harbor Laboratory Archives.)

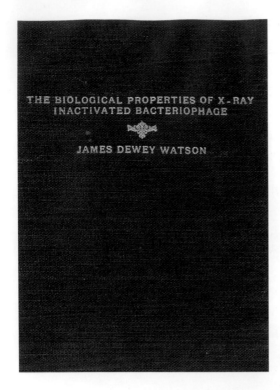

THE BIOLOGICAL PROPERTIES OF X-RAY
INACTIVATED BACTERIOPHAGE

JAMES DEWEY WATSON

Watson's Ph.D. thesis, "The Biological Properties of X-ray Inactivated Bacteriophage," written in 1950. He claims to barely remember what the topic was and that Salvador Luria helped write and rewrite it. (Courtesy of the James D. Watson Collection, Cold Spring Harbor Laboratory Archives.)

intellectual confidence and a sharp evaluation of his teachers. Notwithstanding his high regard for Muller, who used the fruit fly (*Drosophila*) to gain insight into genetics, Watson came to realize that "*Drosophila*'s better days were over and that a new model organism would soon supplant it as the premier tool for studying the gene."[15] This tool was bacteriophages, tiny viruses that accomplish their life cycle in bacteria. So Watson turned to the phage geneticist Salvador Luria for his Ph.D. thesis work.

Watson's thesis addressed an aspect of bacteriophage radiobiology so arcane that he has claimed he does not even remember its title (which was *The Biological Properties of X-ray Inactivated Bacteriophage*). Watson cheerfully confessed that his thesis was mainly rewritten by his mentor Salvador Luria, who was "enjoying his position as an [Italian] immigrant in control of the English language."[16] But he noted, "later I found I could write well when I had a message of importance."[17]

"What I liked about England was that conversation is so important." INTERVIEW WITH JDW, FEBRUARY 9, 2002

Watson received his Ph.D. in 1950 and then obtained a National Research Fellowship to study with Herman Kalckar in Copenhagen. Following a summer in 1950 in Cold Spring Harbor, he spent a year in Copenhagen before moving to Cambridge University's Cavendish Laboratory in 1951 at the age of 23. He again turned to a novelist, Britain's foremost chronicler of English society, noting that "[t]o prepare . . . for my English university life ahead, I read Evelyn Waugh's *Brideshead Revisited.*"[18]

His experiences in Cambridge left their mark in ways beyond the scientific. Watson relished British culture and its opportunities for witty and intelligent conversation:

> *What I liked about England was that conversation is so important. And for conversation to be fun it has to be slightly wicked you know, that is to say, perceptive. You can't just state that everything is good. I liked to listen to conversation. So when I got to Cambridge it was a real eye opener. I thought it was wonderful.[19]*

His accent changed[20] and his writing, too, was influenced:

> *In America you are seldom taught enough about word usage and my English years were essential in my becoming an accomplished writer. A few people here do occasionally use words cleverly, but it is not a national virtue. We are told that if we are sincere, it doesn't matter that we limit ourselves to words that we have known since, say, the sixth grade.[21]*

In 1953, Watson and Francis Crick discovered the double-helical structure of DNA. The paper announcing their model, published in the scientific weekly *Nature*, April 25, 1953, opened with the graceful statement: "We wish to suggest a structure for the salt of deoxyribose nucleic acid (D.N.A). This structure has novel features which are of considerable biological interest."[22] The concluding sentence is frequently quoted as a masterpiece of understatement: "It has not escaped our notice that the specific [base] pairing we have postulated immediately suggests a possible copying mechanism for the genetic material."[23]

Watson was excited about the paper, and, to impress a young lady, he told her that its publication in *Nature* the following week would very likely create a big splash. On a subsequent evening he was mortified to learn that she had searched *Nature* for the article but had only retrieved "a silly note about terminology in bacterial genetics."[24] Watson and others had written this "as a spoof of 'the turgid writings of Joshua Lederberg,'"[25] and this practical joke appeared in the April 18 issue of *Nature*, a week *before* the DNA bombshell.

Watson presented the DNA structure at the June 1953 Cold Spring Harbor Symposium on Viruses, and a paper that he and Crick wrote was published in the proceedings of the Symposium later in the year. He also wrote a full-length manuscript on the DNA structure for the *Proceedings of the Royal Society* in the summer of 1953. With these major scientific accomplishments in hand, he was gaining confidence in his scientific writing style:

> *As I got near the end I began to relax. It was the first time I had put together language of the type that Lawrence Bragg, Max Delbrück, and Linus Pauling had mastered so well.*[26]

In the fall of 1953, Watson moved to Caltech in Pasadena, California. He had long planned this move to pursue postdoctoral work under Max Delbrück, but he was now no longer interested in bacteriophages, having "totally adopted the Cavendish structural biology way of thinking."[27] He was also despondent about exchanging his treasured England for the smog and cultural vapidity of southern California.

"I found I could write when I had a message of importance." JDW, PRESIDENT'S ESSAY, 1998 ANNUAL REPORT

Within two years Watson moved to Cambridge, Massachusetts, to take up a faculty position at Harvard University, and for the next thirteen years he led a productive research laboratory devoted to the study of RNA and protein synthesis. He also introduced the budding disci-

THE STRUCTURE OF DNA

J. D. WATSON[1] AND F. H. C. CRICK
Cavendish Laboratory, Cambridge, England
(Contribution to the Discussion of Provirus.)

It would be superfluous at a Symposium on Viruses to introduce a paper on the structure of DNA with a discussion on its importance to the problem of virus reproduction. Instead we shall not only assume that DNA is important, but in addition that it is the carrier of the genetic specificity of the virus (for argument, see Hershey, this volume) and thus must possess in some sense the capacity for exact self-duplication. In this paper we shall describe a structure for DNA which suggests a mechanism for its self-duplication and allows us to propose, for the first time, a detailed hypothesis on the atomic level for the self-reproduction of genetic material.

We first discuss the chemical and physical-chemical data which show that DNA is a long fibrous molecule. Next we explain why crystallographic evidence suggests that the structural unit of DNA consists not of one but of two polynucleotide chains. We then discuss a stereochemical model which we believe satisfactorily accounts for both the chemical and crystallographic data. In conclusion we suggest some obvious genetical implications of the proposed structure. A preliminary account of some of these data has already appeared in Nature (Watson and Crick, 1953a, 1953b).

I. Evidence for the Fibrous Nature of DNA

The basic chemical formula of DNA is now well established. As shown in Figure 1 it consists of a very long chain, the backbone of which is made up of alternate sugar and phosphate groups, joined together in regular 3′ 5′ phosphate di-ester linkages. To each sugar is attached a nitrogenous base, only four different kinds of which are commonly found in DNA. Two of these—adenine and guanine—are purines, and the other two—thymine and cytosine—are pyrimidines. A fifth base, 5-methyl cytosine, occurs in smaller amounts in certain organisms, and a sixth, 5-hydroxy-methyl-cytosine, is found instead of cytosine in the T even phages (Wyatt and Cohen, 1952).

It should be noted that the chain is unbranched, a consequence of the regular internucleotide linkage. On the other hand the sequence of the different nucleotides is, as far as can be ascertained, completely irregular. Thus, DNA has some features which are regular, and some which are irregular.

A similar conception of the DNA molecule as a long thin fiber is obtained from physico-chemical analysis involving sedimentation, diffusion, light scattering, and viscosity measurements. These techniques indicate that DNA is a very asymmetrical structure approximately 20 A wide and many thousands of angstroms long. Estimates of its molecular weight currently center between 5×10^6 and 10^7 (approximately 3×10^4 nucleotides). Surprisingly each of these measurements tend to suggest that the DNA is relatively rigid, a puzzling finding in view of the large number of single bonds (5 per nucleotide) in the phosphate-sugar back-

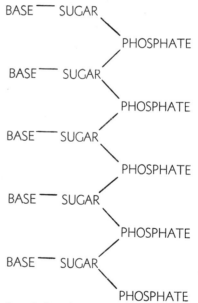

FIGURE 1. Chemical formula (diagrammatic) of a single chain of desoxyribonucleic acid.

[1] Aided by a Fellowship from the National Foundation for Infantile Paralysis.

[123]

Watson presented a paper on the double-helical structure of DNA at the 1953 Symposium on Quantitative Biology shortly after the publication of the Watson–Crick paper in *Nature*. The first page of the published paper, coauthored again with Crick, is shown here. (Reprinted from the 1953 *Cold Spring Harbor Symposium on Quantitative Biology*. Courtesy of Cold Spring Harbor Laboratory Press.)

Watson in his office at Harvard University in the late 1960s. (Courtesy of the James D. Watson Collection, Cold Spring Harbor Laboratory Archives.)

pline of molecular biology to undergraduate students in a new Harvard course. An unorthodox but very committed teacher, Watson began refining his lecture notes with the idea of creating a textbook. The writing of this book interrupted initial efforts he had made toward writing an account of the discovery of the double helix. The textbook *Molecular Biology of the Gene* was published in 1965 and comprehensively documented the discipline of molecular biology for the first time.[28] Its design, structure, and clarity would unalterably change the landscape of textbook publishing in biology.

By the 1960s molecular biology had changed a great deal and much of the work from the 1930s and 1940s that formed its foundation was in danger of being forgotten. *Phage and the Origins of Molec-*

Phage and The Origins of Molecular Biology

Edited by

JOHN CAIRNS
Cold Spring Harbor Laboratory

GUNTHER S. STENT
University of California

JAMES D. WATSON
Harvard University

Cold Spring Harbor Laboratory
of Quantitative Biology
1966

Phage and the Origins of Molecular Biology was a collection of essays by scientists who were strongly influenced by the work of Max Delbrück. The book was presented to Delbrück on the occasion of his 60th birthday. The editors write in the Preface, "Besides paying homage to Delbrück as a prime mover and arbiter of nascent molecular biology, this book is an attempt to write a history of a bygone age and put on record the network of interactions, folklore, and method of operation of the Phage Group that had Delbrück as its focal point." John Cairns, Gunther Stent, and Watson were the editors of the book, published in 1966 by the Cold Spring Harbor Laboratory of Quantitative Biology, as it was then called.

ular Biology,[29] edited by Watson, Gunther Stent, and John Cairns and published by Cold Spring Harbor Laboratory in 1966, contained 35 essays written by many of the pioneers. Conceived as a tribute to Max Delbrück on his 60th birthday, the book was hailed as an important document in the history of biology.[30] It quickly became "required reading for every student of experimental biology . . . [who] will sense the smell and rattle of the laboratory."[31] John Cairns wrote in the preface of an expanded edition published in 1992 that "like many ideas in molecular biology, the idea for the book came from Jim Watson."[32]

"... a good story which the public would enjoy knowing." JDW LET-
TER TO FHC, SEPTEMBER 1966

In 1962 the Nobel Prize for Physiology or Medicine was awarded
to Watson, Francis Crick, and Maurice Wilkins for their discovery of
the structure of DNA. The fundamental importance of this discovery
was affirmed by the mid-1960s, making the timing right for the publication of the book that Watson had been working on for some
years—*The Double Helix: A Personal Account of the Discovery of the
Structure of DNA.*[33] This book was published in 1968 and with it Watson achieved public recognition and professional notoriety. *The Double Helix* has been published in many editions since and has been
translated into over 20 languages (including Thai, Latvian, and, most
recently, Hindi). It has sold more than a million copies and was ranked
seventh in a list of the best 100 nonfiction works published in the English language in the entire 20th century.[34]

"Producing books was already deep in my system . . ." JDW, INTRO-
DUCTION TO LETTERS PRESENTED TO NANCY FORD, JANUARY 30, 1997

In 1968, Watson became Director of the Cold Spring Harbor Laboratory, Cold Spring Harbor, New York, an institution he had first visited as a graduate student in the late 1940s and returned to many
times. The Laboratory occupies a special place in the scientific community, performing internationally recognized basic research in molecular biology and welcoming thousands of scientists and students who
attend the scientific conferences, workshops, and courses held there
each year. From the beginning of his tenure, Watson devoted enormous energy and resources to promoting the best scientific research.
But his passion for books and his interest in educating scientists and
students had particular expression in the guidance and direction he
gave to the Laboratory's publishing activities.

Since 1933, the Laboratory had convened annual Symposia on
Quantitative Biology on subjects of broad interest in biology, and these

COLD SPRING HARBOR SYMPOSIA
ON QUANTITATIVE BIOLOGY

VOLUME XXXVI

STRUCTURE AND FUNCTION
OF PROTEINS AT THE
THREE-DIMENSIONAL LEVEL

COLD SPRING HARBOR LABORATORY
1972

Watson initiated many book projects when he became Director of the Cold Spring Harbor Laboratory. The Symposia proceedings, first published in 1933, were originally the only publication of the Laboratory. This volume on Proteins, published in 1972, was dedicated to Sir Lawrence Bragg (*pictured above*).

proceedings were published in book form. In the 1950s and 1960s, these meetings became events of extraordinary significance for the new discipline of molecular biology and the published proceedings became a cornerstone of its rather small literature. Watson understood both the uniqueness of these volumes as a record of science and their financial benefit to an impoverished institution, and he set about adding more books to the Laboratory's publishing program[35]:

> *Producing books was already deep in my system and if the Lab published more books, our publishing profit should only increase at a time when the Lab was, to say the least, strapped for cash. . . . With the right choice of topics and editors, each [meeting] might generate intellectually valuable and profitable books.*[36]

A monograph series that emerged in the early 1970s had its origins in meetings held at the Laboratory. The first monograph published was

The Lactose Operon. Watson would prevail upon an authoritative and persuasive person in the field to commission articles for a book and edit them, a process that resulted in a series of classic works that are still valued today.[37]

Watson also extended the impact of the Laboratory's practical courses by initiating the publication of manuals for the techniques that were taught. In the Foreword to the first of these publications, *Experiments in Molecular Genetics*, a manual for bacterial genetics published in 1972,[38] Watson commented dryly that the author, Jeffrey Miller, was "old enough to be a master in [the] field, yet . . . too young to know how much work is necessary to turn out a good book."[39] In 1980, Watson gave Tom Maniatis and others the opportunity to run a gene cloning course at Cold Spring Harbor and persuaded them to write a manual that, more than any other publication, became responsible for putting recombinant DNA technology into the hands of scientists around the world.[40] With sales of more than 60,000 copies in its first edition alone, the manual gave publishing at the Laboratory greater financial significance and a new prominence in the wider scientific community.

The Lab's publishing program expanded in 1987 with the launch of *Genes & Development*, the first of several journals, and by 1988, publishing activities at the Lab had been formally constituted as Cold Spring Harbor Laboratory Press under a newly appointed Executive Director. But despite the increasing size of the Laboratory and Watson's growing involvement with the Human Genome Project (he was appointed Associate Director for the NIH Human Genome Program in 1988 and Director of the National Center for Human Genome Research in 1989), he continued to be an important source of ideas for books and suggestions for the right people to be recruited as authors and editors.

Watson had long dreamed of the development and publication at the Laboratory of innovative textbooks for undergraduate students, an activity that demands specialized talents and considerable financial risk. In 2001, Cold Spring Harbor Laboratory Press formally initiated a textbook program and among its first fruits is a new edition of Watson's classic *Molecular Biology of the Gene*.

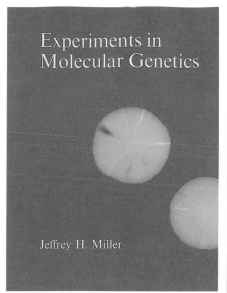 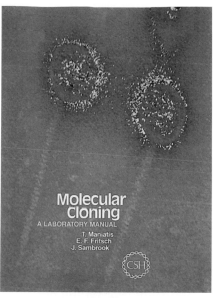

Experiments in Molecular Genetics, published in 1972, was an early success in Cold Spring Harbor Laboratory's publishing program. *Molecular Cloning: A Laboratory Manual,* first published in 1982, was a practical manual of techniques with explanations about how they had been developed and how they had evolved. The manual became a mainstay of molecular biology. A third edition was published in 2001.

In the years of his directorship, Watson also contributed essays to the Laboratory's *Annual Report* that scrutinized the impact of science on society, in particular the many ethical and political implications of recombinant DNA technology and the Human Genome Project. These essays have uncommon style and depth, sometimes combative, at other times reflective, but always thought-provoking and written with a deceptive simplicity.

"As scientists, we shall have to spend more time educating the public." JDW, DIRECTOR'S REPORT, 1976 ANNUAL REPORT, P. 14

The recombinant DNA controversy of the 1970s was the subject of a lively and authoritative book, *The DNA Story: A Documentary History of Gene Cloning,*[41] published in 1981 by Watson and John Tooze of the European Molecular Biology Organization. It concluded with an extended summary of the main scientific advances made possible by recombinant DNA procedures. University instructors told Watson that this section should be "expanded to serve as a supplement to texts written before the recombinant DNA revolution."[42] In response, Watson and Tooze, with David Kurtz, wrote *Recombinant DNA: A Short Course*,[43] published in 1982, consisting of 18 chapters on the basic biology of genes and DNA and explanations of state-of-the-art techniques for DNA work in the laboratory.

The success of *Molecular Biology of the Gene* inspired a larger biology textbook, *Molecular Biology of the Cell*,[44] first published in 1985. Though last in the alphabetical listing of six authors, Watson initiated the book, recruited the authors, and helped write much of it.[45] Like *Molecular Biology of the Gene*, *Molecular Biology of the Cell* was a huge success and continues to enjoy enormous popularity.

In 2000, Watson published a collection of 25 of his essays entitled *A Passion for DNA: Genes, Genomes, and Society.*[46] Included were the best of his Director's Reports, articles written for *Time* magazine, *Nature, New Scientist,* and *The New York Times Magazine,* as well as unpublished material touching upon Watson's own background, which he dubbed "autobiographical flights."[47]

Long in the making, a second book of autobiography, *Genes, Girls and Gamow: After the Double Helix,*[48] was published in England by Oxford University Press in late 2001 and by A.A. Knopf in the United States a few months later. The book covers Watson's life after leaving Cambridge until his academic appointment at Harvard in 1956, his continuing explorations of the gene, his search for a wife, and his relationship with George Gamow, a celebrated physicist and cosmologist who became interested in genes. The book describes a troubled period in Watson's life that contrasts with the DNA discovery just a few years earlier, and it tries to capture the spirit of his youth without judgment.

To mark the 50th anniversary of the discovery of the double helix in 2003, Watson and Andrew Berry wrote a broadly based commentary on DNA science for the general public, entitled *DNA: The Secret of Life,*[49] which accompanied a five-part PBS television documentary.

Books written by Watson. *Clockwise from bottom: Recombinant DNA: A First Course* (1982); *Molecular Biology of the Gene* (1965); *A Passion for DNA: Genes, Genomes, and Society* (2000); *The DNA Story* (1981); *Molecular Biology of the Cell* (1983, B. Alberts et al.); *Genes, Girls, and Gamow: After the Double Helix* (2002); *The Double Helix: A Personal Account of the Discovery of the Structure of DNA* (1965); and (*in the middle*) *DNA: The Secret of Life* (2003, with Andrew Berry). (Photo credit: Phil Renna.)

"You don't need other writers to tell you how to write." INTERVIEW WITH JDW, FEBRUARY 9, 2002

By long habit Watson writes everything by hand. A left-handed writer, he produces an immaculately tidy but excruciatingly diminutive script that Hermann J. Muller once referred to as "just barely macroscopic."[50] His assistant of many years, Maureen Berejka, is credited as being "the sole inhabitant of Planet Earth capable of interpreting"[51] his handwriting. Watson is a meticulous hoarder of drafts and

Watson in his office at Cold Spring Harbor Laboratory, 2003. He writes everything by hand, left-handed. (Courtesy of the James D. Watson Collection, Cold Spring Harbor Laboratory Archives. Photo credit: Miriam Chua.)

has served future historians well in maintaining a comprehensive archive that now resides at Cold Spring Harbor Laboratory.

Watson says he has never kept a personal diary and has never viewed writing "as a way to express emotions I couldn't communicate otherwise."[52] However, his carefully detailed letters to his parents and friends have functioned as a diary and proved crucial as *aides-mémoires* for his autobiographical writings.

He has never systematically sought the advice of established authors, but he does solicit multiple opinions of work in progress. "I often say something that is politically incorrect," he has said, "So now, generally everything I write at the risk of seeming inappropriate I want someone else to read—to keep me from doing unnecessary harm to

A sample of Watson's "barely microscopic" handwriting. This page is an early, 1997, version of the Preface to *Genes, Girls, and Gamow*. (Courtesy of the James D. Watson Collection, Cold Spring Harbor Laboratory.)

myself."[53] But in the same breath he counsels, "you should never ask people for advice unless you want to take it. That's one of my [writing] rules."[54] Watson's wife Elizabeth, a published architectural historian, is a valued source of literary input.[55]

The main room of the Watson Archive. The James D. Watson Collection, which contains personal papers from 1928 to 2002, is organized into 12 different series. The physical processing of the collection is under way. Researchers may use the materials only in situ. (Photo credit: Melissa Frey.)

Watson admires the essay form. "In the 19th and early 20th centuries people wrote essays routinely. Among scientists, Peter Medawar wrote essays, Lewis Wolpert writes essays. So does Walter Gratzer, and of course, Stephen J. Gould did—in his own form. But, writing essays is now becoming a lost art—because of the modern way of life I suppose."[56]

Watson has offered this advice about writing: "Avoid words like 'probably' or 'possibly.' Tell stories as more certain than they really are. It is better to learn a simple story than to not learn a too complicated one. Those who later want all the details will then have to deal with the exception to the rule. Always learn the rule before the exceptions."[57]

The present Carnegie Library was initially built in 1905 as the first research laboratory of the Carnegie Institution at Cold Spring Harbor. Since 1953, it has been the Laboratory Library. The attic was renovated in 1988 to house the Laboratory Archives. The James D. Watson Collection now occupies the south end of the second floor. (Photo credit: Miriam Chua.)

In his foreword to *The Double Helix*, Sir Lawrence Bragg compared Watson to the 17th-century diarist Samuel Pepys, saying that Watson "writes with a Pepys-like frankness."[58] Bragg's perception applies to much of Watson's writing—he is as candid about himself as he is about others. What Claire Tomalin wrote in her 2002 biography of Samuel Pepys also applies to Watson: "The shamelessness of his self-observation deserves to be called scientific."[59]

Notes

1. J.D. Watson. "Manners," draft manuscript. 2001, 2002. The James D. Watson Collection, Cold Spring Harbor Laboratory Archives.
2. J.D. Watson. "Manners," draft manuscript. 2001, 2002. The James D. Watson Collection, Cold Spring Harbor Laboratory Archives.
3. J.D. Watson. 2001. *Genes, girls and Gamow: After the double helix,* p. 64. Oxford University Press, London.

4. Interview with J.D. Watson, Cold Spring Harbor, New York, February 9, 2002.

5. J.D. Watson. 2000. Striving for Excellence. In *A passion for DNA: Genes, genomes, and society*, p. 119. Cold Spring Harbor Laboratory Press, Cold Spring Harbor, New York.

6. J.D. Watson. 2000. Striving for Excellence. In *A passion for DNA: Genes, genomes, and society*, p. 120. Cold Spring Harbor Laboratory Press, Cold Spring Harbor, New York.

7. J. D. Watson. "Manners," draft manuscript. 2001, 2002. The James D. Watson Collection, Cold Spring Harbor Laboratory Archives.

8. E. Schrödinger. 1944. *What is Life? The Physical Aspect of the Living Cell.* Cambridge University Press, Cambridge, United Kingdom.

9. J.D. Watson. 2000. Succeeding in science: Some rules of thumb. In *A passion for DNA: Genes, genomes, and society*, p. 123. Cold Spring Harbor Laboratory Press, Cold Spring Harbor, New York.

10. 2003. A conversation with James D. Watson. *Sci. Am.*, April, p. 68. Vol. 288(4).

11. J.D. Watson. 2000. Values from a Chicago upbringing. In *A passion for DNA: Genes, genomes, and society*, p. 5. Cold Spring Labratory Press, Cold Spring Harbor, New York.

12. J.D. Watson. 1968. *The double helix. A personal account of the discovery of the structure of DNA*, p. 13. Atheneum Press, New York.

13. H.F. Judson. 1979. *The eighth day of creation. The makers of the revolution in biology*, p. 244. Simon and Schuster, New York.

14. J.D. Watson. "Manners," draft manuscript. 2001, 2002. The James D. Watson Collection, Cold Spring Harbor Laboratory Archives.

15. J.D. Watson. "Manners," draft manuscript. 2001, 2002. The James D. Watson Collection, Cold Spring Harbor Laboratory Archives.

16. J.D. Watson. 1998. President's Essay. In *Cold Spring Harbor Laboratory Annual Report*, p. 3. Cold Spring Harbor Laboratory, Cold Spring Harbor, New York.

17. J.D. Watson. 1998. President's Essay. In *Cold Spring Harbor Laboratory Annual Report*, p. 3. Cold Spring Harbor Laboratory, Cold Spring Harbor, New York.

18. J.D. Watson, personal communication.

19. Interview with J.D. Watson, Cold Spring Harbor, New York, February 9, 2002.

20. J.D. Watson. "Manners," draft manuscript. 2001, 2002. The James D. Watson Collection, Cold Spring Harbor Laboratory Archives.

21. J.D. Watson. 2000. Striving for excellence. In *A passion for DNA: Genes, genomes, and society*, p. 121. Cold Spring Harbor Laboratory Press, Cold Spring Harbor, New York.

22. J.D. Watson and F.H.C. Crick. 1953. A structure for deoxyribonucleic acid. *Nature* **171:** 737–738.

23. J.D. Watson and F.H.C. Crick. 1953. A structure for deoxyribonucleic acid. *Nature* **171:** 737–738.

24. J.D. Watson. 2001. *Genes, girls, and Gamow: After the double helix*, p.15. A.A. Knopf, New York.

25. J.D. Watson. 2001. *Genes, girls, and Gamow: After the double helix*, p.15. A.A. Knopf, New York.

26. J.D. Watson. 2001. *Genes, girls, and Gamow: After the double helix,* p. 30. A.A. Knopf, New York.

27. J. D. Watson. "Manners," draft manuscript. 2001, 2002. The James D. Watson Collection, Cold Spring Harbor Laboratory Archives.

28. J.D. Watson. 1965. *Molecular biology of the gene.* W.A. Benjamin, Inc., New York.

29. J. Cairns, G. Stent, and J.D. Watson, eds. 1966. *Phage and the origins of molecular biology.* Cold Spring Harbor Laboratory of Quantitative Biology, Cold Spring Harbor, New York.

30. *Journal of History of Biology,* quoted in advertising copy for the expanded edition of *Phage and the origins of molecular biology* (1992).

31. *Bioscience,* quoted in advertising copy for the expanded edition of *Phage and the origins of molecular biology* (1992).

32. J. Cairns. 1992. Preface. In *Phage and the origins of molecular biology, expanded edition* (ed. J. Cairns, G. Stent, and J.D. Watson), p. v. Cold Spring Harbor Laboratory Press, Cold Spring Harbor, New York.

33. J.D. Watson. 1968. *The double helix: A personal account of the discovery of the structure of DNA.* Atheneum, New York.

34. *Modern Library | 100 Best Nonfiction.* List compiled by the Editorial Board of the Random House *Modern Library.* At http://www.randomhouse.com/modernlibrary/100bestnonfiction.html.

35. Interview with John Inglis, March 31, 2003.

36. J.D. Watson. January 30, 1997. Anticipating Nancy Ford. Introduction to a collection of letters from authors and editors presented to Nancy Ford.

37. Interview with John Inglis, March 31, 2003.

38. J.H. Miller. 1972. *Experiments in molecular genetics.* Cold Spring Harbor Laboratory, Cold Spring Harbor, New York.

39. J.D. Watson. 1972. Foreword. In *Experiments in molecular genetics* (ed. J.H. Miller), p. vi. Cold Spring Harbor Laboratory, Cold Spring Harbor, New York.

40. Interview with John Inglis, March 31, 2003.

41. J.D. Watson and J. Tooze. 1981. *The DNA story: A documentary history of gene cloning.* W.H. Freeman and Company, San Francisco.

42. J.D. Watson, J. Tooze, and D.T. Kurtz. 1982. Preface. In *Recombinant DNA: A short course,* p. xv. Scientific American Books, New York.

43. J.D. Watson, J. Tooze, and D.T. Kurtz. 1982. *Recombinant DNA: A short course.* Scientific American Books, New York.

44. B. Alberts, D. Bray, J. Lewis, M. Raff, K. Roberts, and J.D. Watson. 1983. *Molecular biology of the cell.* Garland Science Publishing, New York.

45. Bruce Alberts, personal communication, October 4, 2002.

46. J.D. Watson. 2000. *A passion for DNA: Genes, genomes, and society.* Cold Spring Harbor Laboratory Press, Cold Spring Harbor, New York.

47. J.D. Watson. 2000. *A passion for DNA: Genes, genomes, and society,* p. v. Cold Spring Harbor Laboratory Press, Cold Spring Harbor, New York.

48. J.D. Watson. 2001. *Genes, girls and Gamow: After the double helix.* Oxford University Press, London (also published by A.A. Knopf [2001] in the United States).

49. J.D. Watson, with A. Berry. 2003. *DNA: The secret of life.* A.A. Knopf, New York.

50. Attributed to H.J. Muller.

51. J.D. Watson, with A. Berry. 2003. Authors Note. In *DNA: The secret of life,* p. x. A.A. Knopf, New York.

52. J.D. Watson, with A. Berry. 2003. Authors Note. In *DNA: The secret of life,* p. x. A.A. Knopf, New York.

53. Interview with J.D. Watson, Cold Spring Harbor, New York, February 9, 2002.

54. Interview with J.D. Watson, Cold Spring Harbor, New York, February 9, 2002.

55. Interview with J.D. Watson, Cold Spring Harbor, New York, February 9, 2002.

56. Interview with J.D. Watson, Cold Spring Harbor, New York, February 9, 2002.

57. Interview with J.D. Watson, Cold Spring Harbor, New York, February 9, 2002.

58. W.L. Bragg. 1968. Foreword. In *The double helix: A personal account of the discovery of the structure of DNA* (by J.D. Watson), p. ix. Atheneum Press, New York.

59. C. Tomalin. 2002. *Samuel Pepys: The unequalled self,* Prologue, p. xxix. A.A. Knopf, New York.

AUTOBIOGRAPHY

THE DOUBLE HELIX

"I never intended to produce a technical volume aimed only at historians of science." JDW, LETTER TO FHC, OCTOBER 19, 1966

In the Preface to *The Double Helix* Watson wrote, "The thought that I should write this book has been with me almost from the moment the double helix was found."[1] From the outset, Watson saw his book as a story, a tale, not a pedantic historical commentary or a conventional autobiography. He wrote to Francis Crick in October 1966:

> I have always felt that the story of how the interactions of me, you, Maurice [Wilkins], Rosalind [Franklin], [Sir Lawrence] Bragg, Linus Pauling, Peter P[auling], etc., finally knitted into the double helix was a good story which the public would enjoy knowing.[2]

But he never considered writing his story with Crick: "If it had to be a story rather than a history, I was going to write it alone. Besides, writing with Francis? He would have probably dominated it!"[3]

The Double Helix presents the story of an epic adventure. Watson skillfully builds the tension of a momentous event in the making and the central role of two young and talented mavericks of science in a race with their rivals in London and at Caltech. The book teems with characters whose foibles, frailties, and eccentricities are captured by Watson with wit and youthful irreverence.

Crick (*left*) and Watson (*right*) during a walk along the backs at Cambridge University (ca. 1952–1953). Kings College Chapel is in the background. (Courtesy of the James D. Watson Collection, Cold Spring Harbor Laboratory Archives.) The picture first appears in *The Double Helix* before the opening page of Chapter 1. Watson wrote in *The Double Helix:* "From my first day in the lab I knew I would not leave Cambridge for a long time. Departing would be idiocy, for I had immediately discovered the fun of talking to Francis Crick . . . . No obstacle thus prevented me from talking at least several hours each day to Francis."

"My objective from the start was to produce a book as good as The Great Gatsby.*"* JDW, *A PASSION FOR DNA*, P. 120

Watson started writing the first chapter of *The Double Helix* in August 1962. Later that year, the Nobel Prize for Physiology or Medicine was awarded to Watson, Crick, and Maurice Wilkins, an event that encouraged Watson's belief that people would understand why he told the story in the unique way that he did because the discovery was so important.[4]

Watson wrote the first chapter of the manuscript in the late sum-

Watson and Albert Szent-Györgyi, Cape Cod, 1964. (Courtesy of the James D. Watson Collection, Cold Spring Harbor Laboratory Archives.) Watson began writing the first chapters of *The Double Helix* in the summer of 1962 at the home of Albert Szent-Györgyi in Woods Hole, Massachusetts. The Hungarian-born biochemist moved to Woods Hole in 1947, where he established the Institute for Muscle Research. Watson first met him in July 1954.

mer of 1962 in the quiet and tranquility of Albert and Marta Szent-Györgyi's Cape Cod home; chapters 2 and 3 were apparently written the following summer. After laying the project aside, Watson took a sabbatical leave in Cambridge, England, in 1965 and continued drafting chapters, taking the opportunity to validate some of the content with Francis Crick. His most productive writing may have been at Carradale, the Scottish country home of the family of his long time friend Avrion (Av) Mitchison.

"I had the first chapter typed by a very fey girl with incredible cat-like blue eyes." JDW, *A PASSION FOR DNA*, P. 120

The process of writing and revising took several years and produced the numerous handwritten originals, typescript drafts, and rewritten chapters, many with handwritten corrections, stored in the James Watson Papers in the Harvard Archives. These 18 binders of material contain almost as many versions of the manuscript. The title page of the first draft in the first binder reads: "Honest Jim (A Description of a Very Great Discovery)." Several 1966 versions of the manuscript are retitled "Base Pairs." Binder 18 contains a "[p]hotocopy typescript of the July 1, 1967 version as shown to Atheneum [Press]." But even the first draft starts with the sentence: "I have never seen Francis [Crick] in a modest mood."

①

I have never seen Francis in a modest mood. Perhaps in other company he is that way but I have never had reason to think about things of him in this tale. It has nothing to do with the fact that he is now, at 4? quite famous and if he lives equally long, they expand I ad/ have/ have to be considered in the Rutherford, or Bohr, or possibly Einstein category. For when I first met, him, almost totally unknown (at 35) he was equally frank, about the correctness of his approach and the general inability of most other people to think, a simple, much less a tricky problem, though to an elegant solution.

Early (1962) version of the handwritten manuscript of "Honest Jim (A Description of a Very Great Discovery)." Harvard University Press originally agreed to publish the book and the Harvard Archives contains numerous early drafts of the manuscript. This draft shows the famous first sentence already in place.

2—galley—31294—The Double Helix—L

1

I H A V E never seen Francis Crick in a modest mood. Perhaps in other company he is that way, but I have never had reason so to judge him. It has nothing to do with his present fame. Already he is much talked about, usually with reverence, and someday he may be considered in the category of Rutherford or Bohr. But this was not true when, in the fall of 1951, I came to the Cavendish Laboratory of Cambridge University to join a small group of physicists and chemists working on the three-dimensional structures of proteins. At that time he was thirty-five, yet almost totally unknown. Although some of his closest colleagues realized the value of his quick, penetrating mind and frequently sought his advice, he was often not appreciated, and most people thought he talked too much.

Leading the unit to which Francis belonged was Max Perutz, an Austrian-born chemist who came to England in 1936. He had been collecting X-ray diffraction data from hemoglobin crystals for over ten years and was just beginning to get somewhere. Helping him was Sir Lawrence Bragg, the director of the Cavendish. For almost forty years Bragg, a Nobel Prize winner and one of the founders of crystallography, had been watching X-ray diffraction methods solve structures of ever-increasing difficulty. The more complex the molecule, the happier Bragg became when a new method allowed its elucidation. Thus in the immediate postwar years he was especially keen about the possibility of solving the structures of

a

"I have never seen . . . ." Typeset galley proof of the beginning of *The Double Helix*. The first sentence of the book remained virtually unchanged from the first draft of the manuscript. As Watson noted in the brief one-page introduction to the book, " . . . as Francis was the dominant force in shaping my part [in the discovery of the double-helical structure of DNA], I will start the story with him." (Courtesy of the James D. Watson Collection, Cold Spring Harbor Laboratory Archives.)

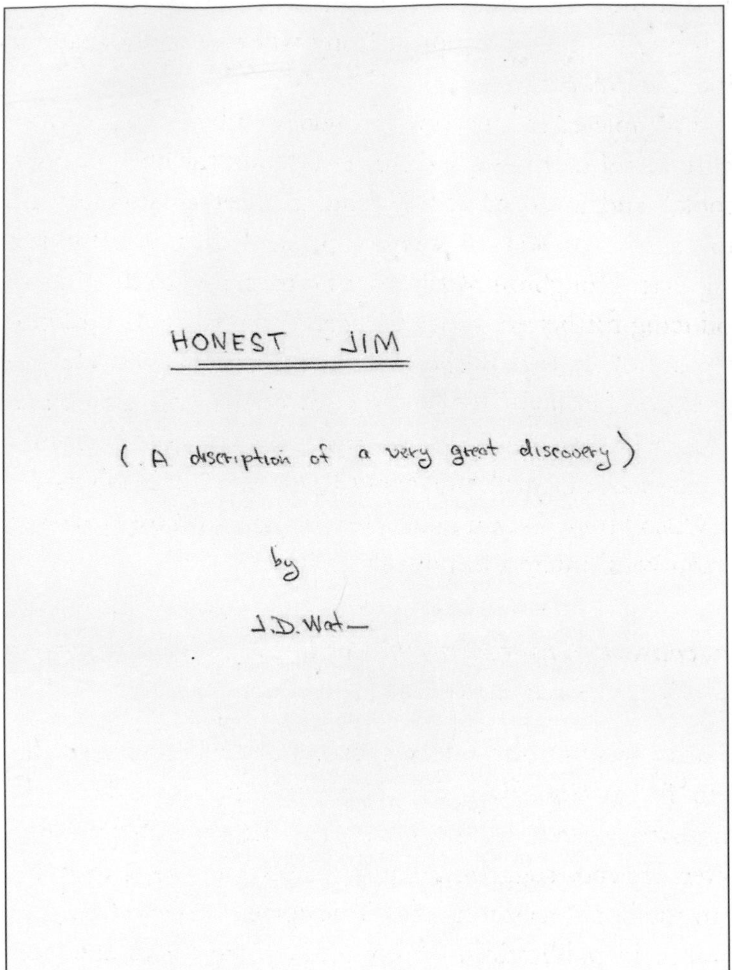

HONEST   JIM

(. A discription of   a very great discovery)

by

J. D. Wat—

Cover page of an earlier draft of the "Honest Jim" manuscript. The final title of the book was arrived at after considering several alternatives, among them "Honest Jim," "Base Pairs," and "The Golden Helix."

Watson's first choice for the title, "Honest Jim," is an echo of both Joseph Conrad's *Lord Jim* and Kingsley Amis's *Lucky Jim*, but in the prologue Watson makes clear that it was reference to a sardonic remark about Watson's character by a member of the rival Kings College research group.[5] This attempt at irony was eventually abandoned for the title *The Double Helix*.

The completed manuscript was reviewed by the editor-in-chief of Houghton Mifflin, but he had concerns about the libelous potential of the book,[6] and arranged for Watson to meet lawyers and hear this opinion firsthand. Watson was not persuaded to alter the text, concluding that "Houghton Mifflin was better suited to the risks involved in producing further editions of Roger Tory Peterson's bird guides."[7]

A more obvious publisher for the manuscript was Harvard University Press. Through the good graces of the evolutionary biologist Ernst Mayr, the draft of "Honest Jim" was forwarded to Tom Wilson, the Director of Harvard University Press. Within 24 hours of receiving it, Wilson told Watson of his great delight with the manuscript and his unequivocal interest in publishing it.

"I was concerned that he might not like the way I first introduced him . . ." JDW, BRAGG'S FOREWORD, IN *A PASSION FOR DNA*, P. 33

Watson was troubled by the prospect of having to show the manuscript to Sir Lawrence Bragg, the Director of the Cavendish Laboratory, whom he had spared in his book no less than any of the other central characters. Friends suggested that Watson invite Bragg to write a foreword to the book, reasoning that if he agreed he would be giving tacit approval to its publication. An opportune moment to approach Bragg arose in the spring of 1966 when Watson, again in England, visited him.

> *Graciously he told me that he wanted me to tell my side of the story, because, given Francis Crick's brilliance, my contributions might well be thought those of a minor contributor. I told him that what he was to read would not be at all what he had asked for. My aim was to write an account where the characters as first portrayed were not always what they later turned out to be. So I was concerned that he might not like the way I first introduced him. If, however, I were to describe his interactions with Francis in any way other than Francis described them to me, my book, as a work of literature, would be badly compromised.[8]*

APR 20 1967

TELEPHONES:
HYDE PARK {0669.
{5716.

THE ROYAL INSTITUTION,
21, ALBEMARLE STREET,
LONDON, W.1.

19 April 1967

Dear Watson,

Many thanks for your letter. It is generous
of you to say that you would understand if I wished
to withdraw my preface, but frankly I should be sorry
to do so! But I should now like to finalise matters
as far as I am concerned and say categorically that
my preface stands on condition that certain changes
set out below are made:

(a) I have rewritten the third paragraph of my
preface ('Finally ... charm of this book'). I wrote
this with the help of John Kendrew and he agrees with
me that in this new form it meets some of Crick's
objections, and is fair.

(b) My other condition is that the account on pages
34 - 36 should be radically changed because much of
it is not true. In particular Kendrew and Perutz
did not tell me they would go if Crick went, and Huxley
never came into the picture at all. I wrote and
scrapped many alternative versions; in the end I
spent the best part of a morning with John Kendrew
mutually confirming our recollections of the event.
The version I enclose is to replace your last paragraph on page 36 ('Max and John ... emerged') and I
want it to go in without alteration. Kendrew and I
wrote it together.

(c) There are some minor alterations. Page 34, 5th
line '... a new manuscript by Sir Lawrence and himself
...'. It should be clear that it was a joint paper
and that Perutz was equally ignorant that Crick had
anticipated any part of the reasoning. I think you
might say on the 10th line 'Bragg and Perutz had not
acknowledged his contribution'. On page 34 second
line from the bottom '... came to him the previous
evening and which Bragg and Perutz subsequently incorporated in the above mentioned paper. While he
was explaining it to Perutz and Kendrew, Crick happened
to join the group. To his considerable annoyance...'.

Bragg's Foreword. Letter to Watson from Sir Lawrence Bragg, April 19, 1967. In it, Bragg reiterated his commitment to writing the Foreword for the book. (Courtesy of the James D. Watson Collection, Cold Spring Harbor Laboratory Archives. Copyright permission granted by the Royal Institution of Great Britain on behalf of the family of Sir Lawrence Bragg.)

A week later, when Watson returned to London, Bragg told him that after some initial displeasure he had come to understand and appreciate Watson's basic intent for the book and he had agreed to write the Foreword. He also acknowledged that such an action would

Foreword by Sir Lawrence Bragg

THIS ACCOUNT of the events which led to the solution of the structure of DNA, the fundamental genetical material, is unique in several ways. I was much pleased when Watson asked me to write the foreword.

There is in the first place its scientific interest. The discovery of the structure by Crick and Watson, with all its biological implications, has been one of the major scientific events of this century. The number of researches which it has inspired is amazing; it has caused an explosion in biochemistry which has transformed the science. I have been amongst those who rave pressed the author to write his recollections while they are still fresh in his mind, knowing how important they would be as a contribution to the history of science. The result has exceeded expectation. The latter chapters, in which the birth of the new idea is described so vividly, are drama of the highest order; the tension mounts and mounts towards the final climax. I do not know of any other instance where one

v

Typeset galley proof of the Foreword by Sir Lawrence Bragg. (Courtesy of the James D. Watson Collection, Cold Spring Harbor Laboratory Archives.)

obviate any consideration of suing for libel—a major turning point for Watson in his plans to have the manuscript published.

Years later, writing about Bragg's Foreword to *The Double Helix*, Watson paid tribute to Bragg's role:

> *In retrospect I do not know whether I would have had the courage to see the publication of* The Double Helix *through to its end without Sir Lawrence's backing . . . .* [9]

"I do not consider my book defamatory in the slightest toward you . . ." JDW, LETTER TO FHC, OCTOBER 19, 1966

Meanwhile Watson sent his "final" draft to Crick, mainly for comments about its factual accuracy. But Crick let it be known that he did not like "Honest Jim" as a title, its implication being that Watson alone

19 October 1966

Dr. Francis Crick
M.R.C. Unit for Molecular Biology
The Medical School
Hills Road
Cambridge, England

Dear Francis,

I am naturally disappointed in your letter of October 10, 1966. Let me comment on several of the points you raise.

(1) Your argument that my book contains far too much gossip and not enough intellectual comments misses entirely what I have tried to do. I never intended to produce a technical volume aimed only at historians of science. Instead, I have always felt that the story of how the interactions of me, you, Maurice, Rosalind, Bragg, Linus Pauling, Peter P., etc., finally knitted into the double helix was a very good story which the public would enjoy knowing. Moreover, since the discovery was one of the great moments in the science of this century, I believe the argument can be made that the general public has a right to know how it all happened. Thus, I tried to write it in such a way that it could be understood by the large audience of intelligent people who would like to read something about how science occurs but who do not have the technical competence to get thrown at them problems, like the strength and specificity of ionic bonds, etc.

(2) Someday, perhaps you or Maurice, but if not, some graduate student in search of a Ph.D. will write a balanced scholarly historical work which takes into account all of the relevant facts, many discovered by me only after the structure came out. Since this was not my purpose, I should not be blamed for not doing so. Quite purposefully I tried to recreate my first impressions of you, Bragg, Cambridge, etc., because only in this way could I try and tell people how our brand of science was done.

(3) I do not consider my book defamatory in the slightest toward you. You have a strong personality, which cannot be avoided if one is to write how you do science. In the early Cambridge days, there were people who thought you talked too much for what they considered your limited ability and insight. But as they were all wrong, I cannot see what harm it does to say that your amazingly productive career

Watson's letter to Francis Crick, October 19, 1966, in response to Crick's criticism of the manuscript, commenting on the points he raised. Countering the third point, he writes, "I do not consider my book defamatory in the slightest toward you. You have a strong personality, which cannot be avoided if one is to write how you do science." Watson concludes: "Thus it is my serious hope that you will gentlemanly, though obviously not enthusiastically, accept its publication and that the ugly spectacle of a Crick-Watson duel will not ooze out into the public world." (Courtesy of the James D. Watson Collection, Cold Spring Harbor Laboratory Archives.) (*Continued on facing page.*)

was hawking the honest truth.[10] Watson changed the title to "Base Pairs"—from the pairing of the bases adenine (A) with thymine (T), and cytosine (C) with guanine (G)—but Crick liked that no better, replying that "everybody will identify the two of us as at least one of the pairs, and I do not see why I should have a book published in which I am described as 'base'."[11] Watson replied to Crick, acknowledging that Harvard University Press also did not like "Base Pairs," favoring "The Golden Helix" or "The Double Helix." He asked Crick if he would accept either alternative.[12]

In the fall of 1966, another revision was forwarded to Crick and to several other players in Watson's tale. Each was asked to sign accompa-

always did not have the support of everyone. In this you are not at all unique, for often being successful demands stating that the work and approaches of the past are outdated. Personally, as you know well, I almost never could hear you speak too much because of the creative intelligence and common sense you brought to bear upon almost everything which interested me.

(4) My view that the book is not in the slightest defamatory toward you has been shared by all of the fifty or so people who have so far read the final draft or one of the earlier versions. About half of these people know you, and like you. None of them have encouraged me not to publish, in fact, just the opposite. Exactly the same favorable impressions have come from a fairly diverse group of reasonable people, who are completely out of science (e.g., the MIT economist Paul Samuelson, the new head of our new Kennedy Institute of Politics, Dick Neustadt, the head of the Guggenheim Foundation, Gordon Ray, (see enclosed letter) and Carl Kaysen, the former Kennedy staff man now Oppenheimer's successor at Princeton). Each has very strongly urged me to publish in virtually the form shown to you.

(5) I am particularly pleased that Harvard University Press intends to publish it, for it confirms my belief that I have not turned out a low-grade compendium of unnecessary gossip. Indeed, I hope that it may be judged a serious literary effort, to which I can feel satisfied about having devoted approximately a year in writing and final preparation in a form suitable for publication.

(6) I feel most firmly that the book should be published soon, not condemned to an underground existence which would automatically generate the impression that some unprintable scandal exists which a variety of people would like to keep quiet. I strongly believe that its publication will reveal to the world that science can be fun and will let a small section of the youth of this world grow up hoping that they can do science in the manner of our early Cambridge days.

Thus it is my serious hope that you will gentlemanly, though obviously not enthusiastically, accept its publication and that the ugly spectacle of a Crick-Watson duel will not ooze out into the public world.

With the usual best regards to Odile,

Yours sincerely,

J. D. Watson

JDW:eob

(Continued from facing page.)

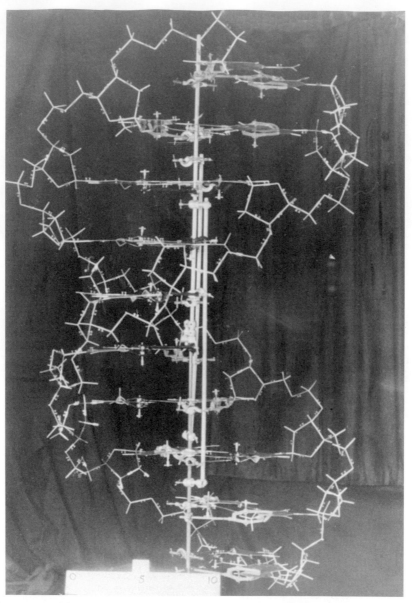

The structure. The original model of the double helix structure, built by Watson and Crick with assistance from the machine shop at Cavendish Laboratory, which supplied the components. In building this model, Watson and Crick were trying to understand what kind of structure could project the X-ray diffraction pattern of crystallized DNA, shown in the now famous photograph taken by Rosalind Franklin. (Photograph courtesy of the James D. Watson Collection, Cold Spring Harbor Laboratory Archives.)

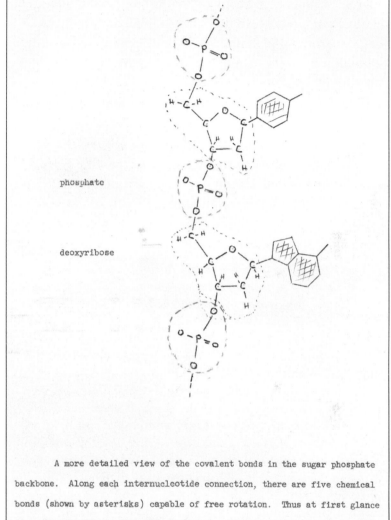

phosphate

deoxyribose

A more detailed view of the covalent bonds in the sugar phosphate backbone. Along each internucleotide connection, there are five chemical bonds (shown by asterisks) capable of free rotation. Thus at first glance it would seem likely that this backbone could fold up into an almost infinite number of configurations. In a regular helix, however, all the internucleotide configurations are identical. Thus by assuming that we would find a helix, we strongly restricted the number of possible models that we would have to consider.

Hand-drawn diagram of a portion of DNA. Watson often drew very good preliminary diagrams for figures used in his books. (Courtesy of the James D. Watson Collection, Cold Spring Harbor Laboratory Archives.)

nying legal documents indicating their willingness to allow Harvard University Press to publish the manuscript. But in early October, Crick again wrote to Watson, this time objecting strenuously to the book's publication.

What prompted Crick to revise his opinion of the manuscript so dramatically in a few short weeks is not clear, even to Watson. Perhaps Crick, having heard Wilkins's and Kendrew's negative responses, was converted from ambivalence to opposition. Through their lawyers, Wilkins and Crick now communicated directly with Nathan Pusey, the President of Harvard, threatening legal action. Nevertheless, these legal threats did not state the opinion that Watson's book was libelous.

Watson lost no time in responding to Crick's letter of early October 1966, expressing his disappointment at its tone and content:

> I do not consider my book defamatory in the slightest toward you. You have a strong personality, which cannot be avoided if one is to write [about] how you do science. In the early Cambridge days, there were people who thought you talked too much for what they considered your limited ability and insight. But as they were all wrong, I cannot see what harm it does to say that your amazingly productive career always did not have the support of everyone. . . .
>
> I feel most firmly that the book should be published <u>soon</u>, not condemned to an underground existence which would automatically generate the impression that some unprintable scandal exists which a variety of people would like to keep quiet. I strongly believe that its publication will reveal to the world that science can be fun and will let a small section of the youth of this world grow up hoping that they can do science in the manner of our early Cambridge days.[13]

"None of them has encouraged me not to publish . . ." JDW, LETTER TO FHC, OCTOBER 19, 1966

The list of colleagues to whom Watson sent copies of "Honest Jim" reads like a *Who's Who* in molecular biology. A lengthy letter from cancer researcher George Klein of the Karolinska Institute, Sweden, in

February 1967 provided a cogent analysis of *The Double Helix* and concluded:

> *I think it requires very great courage and very strong motivation to publish this book. If it is published, I think it will be unique for a long time to come. If it can not be published, this will prove that the homo scientificus is not yet ready to view himself from the outside, as an object, or even try to do so, and cannot use the same liberal philosophy of science as a series of approximations, when he is describing himself, as in other contexts. The emotional barrier, it will have to be concluded, is just too strong to be penetrated. Perhaps it always will be. It is exhilarating and encouraging, however, that you should try to pierce through it.[14]*

Writing to John Kendrew, the preeminent English X-ray crystallographer, John Desmond Bernal commented:

> *It is an astonishing production. I could not put it down. Considered as a novel of the history of science, as it should be written, it is unequalled. . . . It raises many vital problems, not only about the structure of DNA but about the mechanism of scientific discovery which he shows up in a very bad light.[15]*

A letter from the influential editor of *Nature*, John Maddox, written to Watson in early April 1967 also expressed admiration for the manuscript, and caution about reaction to its publication, concluding

> *I admire the book immensely and think that its publication will be a public service. I also think that you will have to barricade yourself in for six months or so after it appears.[16]*

Peter Pauling showed the manuscript to his father, Linus Pauling, who wrote an angry letter to Tom Wilson at Harvard University Press calling it "a disgraceful example of malevolence and egocentricity."[17] Pauling also wrote to Watson, though in a far less vitriolic tone, acknowledging conceptual errors that led him to propose an incorrect (three-stranded instead of two-stranded) model for the structure of DNA, but agreeing with Bragg that the manuscript should be published. However, he took issue with aspects of Watson's criticism:

INST. FÖR TUMÖRBIOLOGI
KAROLINSKA INSTITUTET
STOCKHOLM 60

DEPT. OF TUMOR BIOLOGY   Stockholm, February 24, 1967
KAROLINSKA INSTITUTET
STOCKHOLM 60

Professor J.D. Watson
Department of Biology
Harvard University
Cambridge, Mass. 02136
USA

Dear Jim,

    I have now finished reading the manuscript of your book. I am sorry that
it took such a long time, but I wanted to be sure to read it in detail and
times have been even more hectic than usual.

    Quite frankly, I feel that the book is remarkable and even unique in many
respects. Whether it is wise to publish it or not, is, of course, another
matter, and this is entirely up to you to decide.

    Perhaps it is easiest to comment on the book by trying to give an answer
(quite subjective, of course) to several questions.

    One may ask whether this type of book would have the same interest if
written by somebody who is active in science, possesses the necessary sensitivity
and insight, writes well, but has not succeeded in making any major contribution to science. The answer is probably no; one major reason why this book
is of such interest is because it reflects the many seemingly irrelevant,
personal and often quite accidental factors that enter into any major discovery.

    The reverse of this question would be whether a factual and purely scien-
tific description of the events leading to the discovery of DNA structure,
without the subjective inner monologue of your own personal experience would
have the same value as this book. I guess, my own answer would be definitely
no; a mere historical description of this discovery would be just another
academic contribution to the history of science. There are already many such
books and, no matter how clarifying they may be in principle, their interest
is usually quite ephemeral and they rapidly find their way to dusty upper
shelves in libraries.

    How do I perceive your description of your fellow scientists in this
book? Sharp, perceptive, very sensitive, not very analytical, basically human
and friendly, and yet sceptical with a great deal of mental reservations. In
many details profoundly subjective, I am sure, but very honestly so. Looking
at it from the outside, it gives a marvellous and hitherto probably absolutely
unparallelled description of the excitement, the frustration, the greatness
and the smallness of creative research scientists. Herein lies the uniqueness
of the book.

February 24, 1967 letter to Watson from George Klein, cancer researcher at the Karolinska
Institute, Sweden, who read a draft of "Honest Jim." Klein comments, "Quite frankly, I feel
that the book is remarkable and even unique in many respects. Whether it is wise to publish
it or not is, of course, another matter, and this is entirely up to you to decide." (Courtesy of
the James D. Watson Collection, Cold Spring Harbor Laboratory Archives. Reprinted with the
permission of George Klein.)

Professor J.D. Watson   - 2 -   Stockholm, February 24, 1967

How do I perceive your attitude towards yourself? Making every effort to be sincere, many times a little boyish, surprisingly American, profoundly sensitive, immensely lonely and highly alienated. If I may make a guess, the latter two are probably the reasons why you felt that you had to write this book: the hope that written communication can get through where the oral fails. I would fully symphathize with this since I often find oral communication absolutely hopeless in situations where written communication may still work. However, the misunderstandings inherent in written communications should not be underestimated either; this is the next point:

How do I think your fellow scientists and colleagues whose names appear in the book do perceive the description of their own personality and actions, as they are reflected by your experience? I would think that a very small number of them, those who have most insight, humility and modesty (very rare characteristics among creative scientists), may appreciate the book even if they may feel that one small point or another has been misunderstood or misinterpreted by you. I would expect, however, that the vast majority will be outraged and upset, since your frank description will not fit the superego type of image that they like to form of themselves. Some may secretly admit that you may be right in one thing or another but at the same time they may also resent the fact that you have noticed things which they are very keen on conceiling and, even worse, that you want to put this in print. The reaction of the majority must be therefore, unavoidably and quite naturally, a very negative one.

Should you change the book to a major extent if you get comments that are directed by motives like the ones mentioned above? I think that, unless there are some clear misunderstandings or misinterpretations of detail, trying to please everybody would absolutely castrate the book. My opinion is that the book should be essentially printed as it is, or not at all.

I think it requires very great courage and very strong motivation to publish this book. If it is published, I think it will be unique for a long time to come. If it can not be published, this will prove that the homo scientificus is not yet ready to view himself from the outside, as an object, or even try to do so, and cannot use the same liberal philosophy of science as a series of approximations, when he is described himself, as in other contexts. The emotional barrier, it will have to be concluded, is just too strong to be penetrated. Perhaps it will always be. It is exhilarating and encouraging, however, that you should try to pierce through it.

Many thanks again for letting me see this book which I profoundly enjoyed, more so than many other readings since a long period of time. Do let me know how it fares. Please also let me know whether you want the manuscript back or not. It has been shown to nobody except to Eva.

Warmest greetings (I still recall with pleasure that Sunday lunch at your and your father's home),

Very sincerely yours,

George Klein

GK/AL

(Continued from facing page.)

BIRKBECK COLLEGE
(UNIVERSITY OF LONDON)
MALET STREET
W.C.1

LANGHAM 6622

DEPARTMENT OF CRYSTALLOGRAPHY
PROFESSOR J. D. BERNAL, M.A., F.R.S.

Dr. J. C. Kendrew, F.R.S.,
M.R.C. Laboratory of Molecular Biology,
Hills Road,
CAMBRIDGE.   20th December, 1966.

Dear Kendrew,

    I have now read the book entitled <u>Base Pairs</u> by Watson.
It is an astonishing production, I could not put it down.
Considered as a novel of the history of science, as it should
be written, it is unequalled. It is as exciting as Martin
Arrowsmith but has the advantage of being about the history
of a real and very important discovery. It raises many vital
problems, not only about the structure of DNA but about the
mechanism of scientific discovery which he shows up in a very
bad light. I am astonished that it is allowed to be published.
In England it would be libellous in many places, but I imagine
U.S. laws are different.

    As someone who comes into it by implication but not directly -
I never met Watson before the discovery but if I had I could have
told him quite a lot - what impressed me most is that he did not
know, and apparently never tried to find out, what had been done
already in the subject. He is particularly unfair on the
contribution of Rosalind Franklin and does not mention her
projection of the helical DNA structure showing the external
position of the phosphate groups. I need not mention the complete
absence of a reference to the work of Furberg which contains all
the answers to the structure except one vital one - the double
character of the chain and the hydrogen bond base pair linkage.
Effectively, all the essentials of the structure were present in
Astbury's original studies, including the negative birefringence
and the 3.4 Å piling of the base groups. I should add in my own
defence that my weakness was in what he calls the English habit
of respect for other peoples work. There was a tacit understanding.
I dealt with biological crystalline substances and Astbury dealt
with messy substances. Nucleic acids came clearly in the second
category. It was not that I considered them unimportant but it
was not my responsibility. I was certainly wrong in this. Astbury
was quite clearly incapable of working out the structure. The
genetic importance of DNA was apparent to me long before from the
work of Caspersson which, Watson hardly mentions. Watson and
Crick did a magnificent job but in the process were forced to
make enormous mistakes. which they had the skill to correct in time.
The whole thing is a disgraceful exposure of the stupidity of
great scientific discoveries. My verdict would be the lines of
Hilaire Belloc'

       "And is it true? It is not true!
       And if it was it wouldn't do."

In his December 20, 1966 letter to John Kendrew, a molecular biologist at Trinity College, Cambridge University, J.D. Bernal, the Irish crystallographer, also at Cambridge, describes his reactions to the "Base Pairs" manuscript. (*Continued on facing page.*)

Dr. J. C. Kendrew, F.R.S.   20th December, 1966.

I am sure this publication of Base Pairs will cause a lot of heart-burnings in scientific circles and particularly in England but it makes very good reading and I think it would make an even better film because it is so alive and dramatic.

I will keep it for another few days and then will send it back to you. There is a page missing and another illegibly copied.

I enjoyed our conversation the other day very much.

                    Yours sincerely,

                    J. D. Bernal

                    J. D. Bernal.

"It is an astonishing production, I could not put it down," Bernal writes, but notes, "I am astonished that it is allowed to be published." (Courtesy of the James D. Watson Collection, Cold Spring Harbor Laboratory Archives.)

NATURE

Editorial and Publishing Offices

MACMILLAN (JOURNALS) LIMITED

LITTLE ESSEX STREET, LONDON, W.C.2

Telephone: TEMPLE BAR 6633   Telegrams: PHUSIS LONDON WC 2

JM/MS/P-4133   13th April 1967

Professor J.D. Watson
Harvard University
Biological Laboratories
16 Divinity Avenue
CAMBRIDGE, MASSACHUSETTS 02138

Dear Watson:

This letter is to do three things - to explain about
Ptashne's paper, to thank you for sending the book and
to give you some preliminary comments on it, and to hope
that we can indeed meet at some point in the next few
weeks.

Naturally the cable you sent on March 17th saying that you
did not think Ptashne would be able to make the April 8th
issue led me to think that he had gone back to the bench to
do some more experiments.   Presumably at some stage he
telephoned and found that his manuscript had not arrived -
certainly we had no record of having had a letter, although
one of the people who may have dealt with this is on holiday
this week so I cannot check that.   And then of course your
covering letter turned up last Monday with the manuscript
and I assume that it must have come by seamail.   But fortu-
nately, thanks to Ptashne's running around in the snow, the
air version turned up, and has been printed this week, and
I hope I am writing in thinking that this is about as speedy
a publication as there would have been even if it had been
sent to an ordinary journal and had travelled airmail.   By
the way, I hope that Gilbert's piece will soon be ready and
that he too will be tempted to send it to us.

I have read the book with the greatest interest and propose
reading it again before finally returning it to you.   I
would like you to regard what follows as a preliminary
opinion.   For one thing, there is nothing in it which could
be thought of as libellous, at least in my opinion.   Reports
of the book that I had heard from other people had led me to
expect something much more dodgy.   I also find the book not
merely enthralling but a valuable and sensitive account of
the way in which interactions between people can influence

                                               (cont'd.)

Letter from John Maddox, the influential editor of *Nature*, April 13, 1967, cautioning about the potential reaction to the manuscript. Maddox writes, "I have read the book with the greatest interest . . . I . . . find the book not merely enthralling but a valuable and sensitive account of the way in which interactions between people can influence the course of important events." (Courtesy of the James D. Watson Collection, Cold Spring Harbor Laboratory Archives. Reprinted with the permission of Sir John Maddox.)

NATURE

Editorial and Publishing Offices

MACMILLAN (JOURNALS) LIMITED
LITTLE ESSEX STREET, LONDON, W.C.2

Telephone: TEMPLE BAR 6633   Telegrams: PHUSIS LONDON WC2

Professor J.D. Watson   - 2 -   13th April 1967

the course of important events.   In other words I would
like to see it published.   At the same time, it seems to
me that publication will entail problems of two kinds
which will affect you and not your readers.   In the first
place, it would be unreasonable to expect that the people
mentioned in the book would retain the same kind of personal
relationship with you after publication.   Everything will
of course depend on who they are and what they are.   The
second problem is one of journalistic ethics.   In ordinary
newspaper reporting, it is considered unfair to write down
what a man says unless he knows that what he is saying is
likely to be reported.   Books are different - and have been
even before William Manchester came along - and I would agree
with those who say that, just as political events are of
great public importance and deserve to be described in
detail, so too are scientific events like those you describe.
But there are bound to be people who say that they have been
caught off their guard by your book, and there will be some
kind of controversy about that.   No doubt you have followed
the discussions there have been of Ved Mehta (New Yorker) and
his doings.

Let me say again that I admire the book immensely and think
that its publication will be a public service.   I also think
you will have to barricade yourself in for six months or so
after it appears.   By the way, I would feel bound to send
the book for review to Crick or to Wilkins.   That should be
fun too.

I mentioned on the telephone that I am turning up in Boston
later this month.   We are proposing to have a party at the
Commodore Hotel on the evening of Saturday April 29th and I
hope you would be able to come.   I will let you know times
later.   But I should also like to come and see your lab.
Do you by any chance work on Saturday morning?

With all good wishes,

Yours sincerely,

John Maddox

(Continued from facing page.)

I did not make any mistakes such as you attribute to me. . . . Your whole argument is based upon your own lack of knowledge of the strengths of acids and your erroneous belief that DNA is a strong acid. It is fortunate that you did not need to be right in this matter in order to discover the double-chain helix.[18]

" . . . we have no intention of watering down the effort to show how scientists look at science and at each other." JDW, LETTER TO NICHOLAS THOMPSON, NOVEMBER 10, 1966

Watson and Tom Wilson became increasingly concerned about compromising Nathan Pusey's position as President of Harvard and Wilson eventually came to the unilateral decision that Harvard University Press would not publish Watson's book without express approval from Pusey. Meanwhile, Watson and Wilson agreed that senior editor Joyce Lebowitz should tone down parts of the manuscript. However, in November of 1966, Watson wrote to Nicolas Thompson of the English publisher Weidenfeld and Nicholson, "I assure you, we have no intention of watering down the effort to show how scientists look at science and at each other."[19]

"But there is one unfortunate exception." JDW, EPILOGUE, *THE DOUBLE HELIX*

Joyce Lebowitz suggested that since Rosalind Franklin was no longer alive Watson might consider adding an epilogue to the book that highlighted his relationship with Franklin from a more current perspective, anticipating that among the many controversies the book would arouse, none would rage more bitterly than his portrayal of Rosalind Franklin. In the Epilogue, Watson acknowledged that his initial impressions of Rosalind Franklin, both scientific and personal, were often wrong. And commented that, later,

all traces of our early bickering were forgotten, and we both [Crick and I] came to appreciate greatly her personal honesty and gen-

erosity, realizing years too late the struggles the intelligent woman faces to be accepted by a scientific world which often regards women as mere diversions from serious thinking.[20]

Much has been made of Watson's access to a key photograph that Franklin generated of the X-ray diffraction pattern of DNA and this resurfaced in a new biography of Franklin by Brenda Maddox.[21] In a recent interview Watson commented, "People have said, why didn't you talk to Rosalind later and thank her for seeing the picture? She didn't want to talk about it. She didn't want to talk to coworkers about it."[22] It suffices here to state that Watson and Crick's discovery never interrupted the cordiality of their relationship with Franklin, which endured until her untimely death.

". . . not for a moment have I considered abandoning the publication . . ." JDW, LETTER TO NICHOLAS THOMPSON, MAY 24, 1967

In the early part of 1967, the edited manuscript, still called "Honest Jim," was sent out again to the principal players. Watson offered Sir Lawrence Bragg the opportunity of backing out of his earlier agreement to write the Foreword. Bragg's response was reassuring. Thanking him, Watson commented how pleased he was by Bragg's decision, adding

The innumerable complications which have arisen, of course, have made me wonder at times whether I have bitten off more than I can chew.[23]

The continued objections from Wilkins and Crick remained a complication. Then Wilkins countered with a proposal of his own—that Watson abandon the notion of an independent publication and consider including his manuscript in a formal, comprehensive history of the discovery of the structure of DNA to be written by the English historian of science Robert Olby, then at the University of Pittsburgh.

MEDICAL RESEARCH COUNCIL

Telephone:
Cambridge 48011

LABORATORY OF MOLECULAR BIOLOGY,
UNIVERSITY POSTGRADUATE MEDICAL SCHOOL,
HILLS ROAD,
CAMBRIDGE.

13th April 1967.

Dr J.D. Watson,
Harvard University Biological
  Laboratories,
16 Divinity Avenue,
Cambridge, Mass. 02139,
U.S.A.

Dear Jim,

The new version of Honest Jim is naturally a little better, but my
basic objections to it remain the same as before. They are:

I. The book is not a history of the discovery of DNA, as you claim in
    the preface. Instead it is a fragment of your autobiography
    which covers the period when you worked on DNA.

    I do not see how anybody can seriously dispute this, for the following
      reasons:-

    a) Important scientific considerations, which concerned you at the
        time, are omitted. For example the work of Furberg, which
        established the relative configuration of the sugar and the
        base. There are many other examples.
    b) Such scientific details that are mentioned are referred to rather
        than described. For example, you do not explain exactly why
        you got the water content of DNA wrong, nor make it clear that
        if there had been so little water electrostatic forces were
        bound to predominate. You do not mention that Pauling worked
        from an old X-ray picture of Astbury's which had both the A
        and B pictures on the same photograph. There are many other
        examples.
    c) The thread of the argument is often lost beneath the mass of
        personal details. For example I asked both Bragg and Doty
        the following question. "Since we had realized that 1:1

First page (*above*) of letter from Francis Crick, written April 13, 1967, which contains a long list of objections to the manuscript. The final page (*opposite*) shows that copies of the letter were sent to ten other people involved in the discussion about the book's publication, including Harvard's President Pusey. (Courtesy of the James D. Watson Collection, Cold Spring Harbor Laboratory Archives. Reprinted with the permission of Francis H. Crick.)

Dr J.D. Watson. <ins>13th April 1967</ins>.

There is no reason why your book, as it stands, should not be made available to selected scholars, provided any documents you may have (such as your letters to your mother) which bear on the subject are also made available at the same time.

My objection, in short, is to the widespread dissemination of a book which grossly invades my privacy, and I have yet to hear an argument which adequately excuses such a violation of friendship. If you publish your book now, in the teeth of my opposition, history will condemn you, for the reasons set out in this letter.

I have written separately to Wilson pointing out several cases of factual errors in your latest draft. I enclose a copy of my letter to him.

Yours sincerely,

Francis.

F.H.C. Crick.

Copies to: President Pusey.
Sir Lawrence Bragg.
M.H.F. Wilkins.
L. Pauling.
T.J. Wilson.
J.T. Edsall.
P. Doty.
J.C. Kendrew.
M.F. Perutz.
A. Klug.

(Continued from facing page.)

Crick's response to the revised manuscript, in early April 1967 was a five-page letter to Watson, in which he detailed his basic objections:

> I. *The book is not a history of the discovery of DNA, as you claim in the preface. Instead it is a fragment of your autobiography which covers the period when you worked on DNA. I do not see how anybody can seriously dispute this, for the following reasons: -*
>
>   *a)* *Important scientific considerations, <u>which concerned you at the time</u>, are omitted. . . .*
>
>   *b)* *Such scientific details that are mentioned are referred to rather than described. . . .*
>
>   *c)* *The thread of the argument is often lost beneath the mass of personal details. . . .*
>
>   *d)* *No attempt is made to ask or answer questions which would interest the historian . . .*
>
>   *e)* *Gossip is preferred to scientific considerations. . . .*
>
>   *f)* *Much of the gossip and even some of the science is irrelevant to a history of DNA. . . .*
>
>   *g)* *Absolutely no attempt is made to document your assertions, many of which are not completely accurate because of your faulty memory. . . .*
>
> II. *Considered as autobiography your book is misleading and in bad taste.*
>
>   *a)* *Your book is misleading because it does not in fact accurately convey the atmosphere in which the work was done. . . .*
>
>   *b)* *Your book is in poor taste because of the style. . . .*[24]

Crick suggested that the book either be scrapped and a "proper" history of the subject written, or that the manuscript be put aside for publication either after all the major participants agreed to it or after those who objected were dead.[25] He objected to the widespread dissemination of a book that grossly invaded his privacy.[26]

Nevertheless, Watson decided that he would publish without formal consent from Wilkins and Crick. Harvard's President Pusey let it be known "that for Harvard to publish the book 'would be to take sides in a scientific dispute' and that 'publication by a commercial house would be more appropriate.'"[27] Thus, the Harvard Corporation, the university's ruling body, prevented Harvard University Press from publishing Watson's manuscript despite unanimous support from the faculty body Syndic.

No one was more disappointed than Harvard University Press editor Joyce Leibowitz, who had tirelessly prepared the book for publication and who wrote to Watson saying that the decision not to publish was "one we're sure to regret."[28]

" . . . lots of money that the University would have made went instead to the Athenaeum Press." JDW, *A PASSION FOR DNA*, P. 121

Meanwhile, Tom Wilson had decided to take an early retirement from Harvard University and to join the New York publishing house Atheneum Press. With Watson's enthusiastic consent, Wilson took *The Double Helix* with him.

Editorial Department

HARVARD UNIVERSITY PRESS
79 GARDEN STREET · CAMBRIDGE · MASSACHUSETTS · 02138

May 25, 1967

Professor James D. Watson
10 Appian Way
Cambridge, Massachusetts

Dear Jim:

I think I want to say rather more formally, in writing, how sorry I am that we're not being allowed to publish your book. It's a wretched decision, one we're sure to regret for a long time to come. Others can be generous and understanding about it - myself I just don't feel like accepting it with professional calm, jolly old sportsmanship, and grown-up good grace. Be that as it may, please know that we've all tried very hard and that the entire Press is disappointed. That is cold comfort, I know. But I really do think the manuscript reads better now, after all the work, so perhaps it hasn't been a total loss. Again, a very small comfort.

Short of ten paces at dawn, the situation at Cold Spring Harbor should, I think, be one of an icy ignoring of the presence of Francis Crick. Nonetheless, if worse comes to worst, give him one for me.

My best,

Joyce

Letter to Watson from Joyce Lebowitz, May 25, 1967. Joyce, editor at Harvard University Press, had worked tirelessly on editing the manuscript. Even after it moved to Atheneum, she continued to keep up with the status of its publication and wrote memos to guide the tone of the marketing and publicity for the book. (Courtesy of the James D. Watson Collection, Cold Spring Harbor Laboratory Archives.)

In the early fall of 1967, Atheneum's lawyer rendered an opinion that the manuscript was not libelous but suggested that Watson change (among other phrases) the opening sentence *"I have never seen Francis Crick in a modest mood,"* to the more legally defensible phrase *"I can't remember ever having seen Francis Crick in a modest mood."*[29] He also recommended that "it might be well to indicate casually that Crick's preoccupation with women was not of a nature that led to adultery (if that was the case)."[30] A few months later, lawyers for Weidenfeld and Nicholson in England also concluded that the manuscript was not libelous. So ended the legal discord between Watson and his scientific colleagues.

With publication now certain, Weidenfeld and Nicholson proposed a written endorsement from C.P. Snow, a long-time advocate of the popularization of science. The cover of the British edition of *The Double Helix* contained the comment from Snow:

> *Like nothing else in literature, it gives one the feel of how creative science really happens. It opens a new world for the general non-scientific reader.*[31]

But the promotional copy on the back of the book, composed in-house by Weidenfeld and Nicholson, was a problem:

> *Which winner of the Nobel prize has a voice so loud that it can actually produce a buzzing in the ears?*
> *Who is the top Cambridge scientist who gossips over dinner about the private lives of women undergraduates?*
> *Which eminent English biologist created a scandal at a costume party by dressing up as George Bernard Shaw and kissing all the girls behind the anonymity of a red scraggly beard?*[32]

Watson immediately cabled his disgust with this "disgraceful insult to Crick," demanding that all copies of the dust jacket be destroyed, and threatening immediate suit.[33] Within a few days he was reassured by Weidenfeld and Nicholson and Atheneum Press that his wishes had been followed and steps taken to ensure that no copies would fall into the wrong hands. One of these original dust jackets is preserved in the Watson archives at Cold Spring Harbor Laboratory.

The Double Helix (initially with the subtitle *Being a Personal*

```
                    HARVARD UNIVERSITY
                THE BIOLOGICAL LABORATORIES
                     16 DIVINITY AVENUE
                CAMBRIDGE, MASSACHUSETTS 02138

                                    8 April 1968




Cable:

Thompson

    Double Helix flyjacket disgraceful insult to Francis Crick.

Demand you withdraw all copies and replace with cover showing you

are more than cheap scandalmongers.  Reply immediately.  If necessary

I will bring immediate suit.



                                    Watson



Thompson
Weidenfeld and Nicolson
5 Winsley Street
London, W1, England

NICOBAR, London W1
```

Cable from Watson to Nicholas Thompson of the British publisher Weidenfeld and Nicholson, April 8, 1968, expressing outrage at the wording on the back of the dust jacket. The cover was subsequently changed. The British edition of the book was published shortly after its publication in the United States by Atheneum. (Courtesy of the James D. Watson Collection, Cold Spring Harbor Laboratory Archives.)

Account of the Discovery of the Structure of DNA, a Major Scientific Advance Which Led to the Award of a Nobel Prize) was published by Atheneum in February 1968, and by Weidenfeld and Nicholson in the same year. In subsequent editions, the subtitle was shortened to *A Personal Account of the Discovery of the Structure of DNA*. Immediately preceding its appearance in book form Tom Wilson arranged for *The Double Helix* to be serialized in two parts by *The Atlantic*.

Atheneum launched *The Double Helix* with a luncheon at the Century Club in New York. Victor McElheny, author of a current Watson

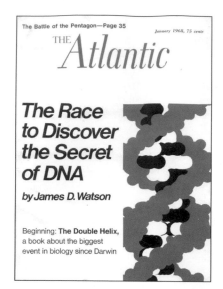 

Covers of *The Atlantic*, January (*left*) and February (*right*) 1968. Tom Wilson had arranged for *The Double Helix* to be serialized in two parts in *The Atlantic*, just before the actual book was published by Atheneum in February 1968. (Courtesy of the James D. Watson Collection, Cold Spring Harbor Laboratory Archives. Reproduced, with permission, from *The Atlantic Monthly*.)

biography and then a journalist, recalls that during his luncheon remarks Watson stated: "The book was intended for 16-year-olds just going into science and wondering what it was like." He also remarked that he was not influenced by C.P. Snow's first novel, *The Search,* about a young physicist and based on the life of J.D. Bernal.

"I'm very, very pleased with the reaction to the book itself . . ."
JDW, LETTER TO NAOMI MITCHISON, FEBRUARY 19, 1968

The Double Helix was extensively reviewed, mainly by scientists in science journals, rather than literary critics.[34] Many ignored Watson's explicitly stated intention to recount the events, the people, and himself as they were in 1951–1953.[35] Dismay was widespread, especially among scientists who valued dispassionate and objective reporting. However, Peter Medawar, in *The New York Review of Books*, predicted that *The Double Helix* "will be an enormous success, and deserves to be so—a classic in the sense that it will go on being read."[36] He was absolutely correct. More than one million copies have been sold and the book has been translated into more than 20 languages. No other story about scientific discovery has reached so large an audience. (In 1987 the story was made into a movie by the BBC, "Life Story," starring Jeff Goldblum as Watson.)

In 1974, the University of Washington Press published the book by Robert Olby called *The Path to the Double Helix: The Discovery of the Structure of DNA*.[37] The chapter "Hunting for the Helix" detailed the events culminating with Watson and Crick's DNA model. Watson wrote to Olby that he "found the 'Hunting for the Helix' section superb and most enjoyed reading it,"[38] and ended with the comment, "My congratulations on a real book."[39] In his Foreword to Olby's book, Francis Crick wrote:

> *Watson's book was really a fragment of his autobiography. Not only did he attempt to describe the discovery of the DNA through the eyes of the young man he was at that time, but he included many lively personal details not strictly essential to his main theme. . . . But then Watson's principal aim was to show that scientists were human, a fact only too well known to scientists themselves but apparently not, at that time, to the general public. Hence the book's enormous success. Even if the science could only be glimpsed it sounded exciting and the gossip was irresistible.*[40]

In 1988, Crick published his own account in *What Mad Pursuit: A Personal View of Scientific Discovery*. In an absorbing chapter entitled "Books and Movies About DNA," he wrote:

> *I found it difficult to take his [Watson's] account seriously. "Who," I asked myself, "could possibly want to read stuff like this?" Little did I know! My years of concentration on the fascinating problems of molecular biology had, in some respects, led me to live in an ivory tower. . . . I now appreciate how skillful Jim was, not only in making the book read like a detective story (several people have told me they were unable to put it down) but also by managing to include a surprisingly large amount of the science, although naturally the more mathematical parts had to be left out.*[41]

The Atheneum's edition of *The Double Helix* (*left*) first came out in February 1968; the British edition (*right*) was published by Weidenfeld and Nicholson shortly thereafter. The Atheneum's burgundy and white cover has an elegant look and the typesetting in the interior is crisp. In the Weidenfeld and Nicholson edition, which must have been photographically reproduced, the type is slightly enlarged and fuzzier. The cover design is in black and white. The original subtitle, "being a personal account of the discovery of the structure of DNA, a major scientific advance which led to the award of a Nobel Prize" was later shortened to "A Personal Account of the Discovery of the Structure of DNA" for subsequent editions. (Photo credit: Phil Renna.)

Not long after *The Double Helix* was published Watson received a note from an inspired young reader to which he replied:

> *Before my book came out, I went through two years of battles with friends who felt I would seriously damage the image and hence the future of science. So a letter like yours makes me feel pleasantly relieved.*[42]

As late as 1977, he responded to a high school senior:

> *I can personally tell you how much I enjoyed your letter about my books [sic]. I find writing a most difficult task and am overjoyed when someone tells me the final result is exciting to read.*[43]

The book's popular appeal accounted for the rapidity with which the acronym "DNA" was translated from the lexicon of science to

UNIVERSITY of PENNSYLVANIA

PHILADELPHIA, PENNSYLVANIA 19104

Department of Chemistry

27 April 1970

Professor James D. Watson
Department of Biology
Harvard University
Cambridge, Mass. 02138

Dear Jim,

Enclosed find the results of the 4th race at Garden State

last Friday. It appears you have achieved the ultimate, having

had a horse named after one of your creations. Note, however,

that although he rallied boldly to gain command" he "tired badly

in the late stages". Is this some kind of message? (Perhaps he

didn't use different maps.)

Yours truly,

Jerry

Jerry Donohue

JD:pm

On April 27, 1970, two years after *The Double Helix* was published, Jerry Donohue sent Watson this note and the accompanying newspaper clipping with the results from the fourth race at Garden State where the horse Double Helix was running. Donohue shared an office at the Cavendish Laboratory in 1953 with Watson, Crick, and Peter Pauling. (Courtesy of the James D. Watson Collection, Cold Spring Harbor Laboratory Archives.)

Wendy Coates
5529 Fifth Ave.
Pittsburgh, Pa. 15232
January 12, 1977
JAN 24 RECD

Dr. James Watson
Department of Biology
Harvard University
Cambridge, Mass.

Dear Dr. Watson

I am a high school senior in Pittsburgh, Pa. Recently, in my Biology class, we were assigned to do a report about a scientist and his discovery.

For the past two or three years, I have been very interested in Genetics. For this reason, and because I was interested in a modern discovery, I chose you as the subject of my report. After reading your book, The Double Helix, it became apparent to me that the life of a scientist is not quite as rigid as I had once expected. I admired your persistence.

Perhaps the one thing which encouraged me was that you, alone, could not accomplish everything and that people were sometimes willing to help.

April 7, 1977

Miss Wendy Coates
5529 Fifth Avenue
Pittsburgh, Pennsylvania   15232

Dear Wendy Coates:

Now that I am back in Cold Spring Harbor, I can personally tell how much I enjoyed your letter about my books. I find writing a most difficult task and am overjoyed when someone tells me the final result is exciting to read.

Yours sincerely,

J. D. Watson
Director

Letter from high school senior Wendy Coates to Watson, January 12, 1977 (*left*) and Watson's response, April 7, 1977 (*right*). When contacted for permission to reprint her letter, Wendy Coates responded: "I remember vividly the day I received the response from Dr. Watson. The fact that he would take the time to answer a high school student, personally, demonstrated that he was an exceptional person in addition to an accomplished scientist. It made a tremendous impression on me at a time when I needed it most. I have since attended medical school and am a medical school professor at UCLA School of Medicine. I am also involved in advancing medical education on a national scale within the specialty of Emergency Medicine (a far cry from Molecular Biology!)." (Courtesy of the James D. Watson Collection, Cold Spring Harbor Laboratory Archive. Reprinted with permission of Wendy Coates.)

Translations of *The Double Helix*. The book has sold more than one million copies and has been translated into more than 23 languages. No other story about scientific discovery has reached so large an audience. (Photo credit: Phil Renna.)

common usage. As geneticist Steve Jones has noted, in an Introduction to a 1996 edition of *The Double Helix*,

> *science, in the public mind, is detached from the people who practice it. Everyone knows about viruses, or the background radiation of the Big Bang, but almost nobody could name the individuals who discovered them. DNA is different and this book is the reason why.*[44]

Notes

1. J.D. Watson. 1968. Preface. In *The double helix: A personal account of the discovery of the structure of DNA*, p. 4. Atheneum Press, New York.
2. J.D. Watson, letter to Francis Crick, October 19, 1966. The James D. Watson Collection, Cold Spring Harbor Laboratory Archives.
3. Interview with J.D. Watson, February 9, 2002, Cold Spring Harbor.

4. Interview with J.D. Watson, February 9, 2002, Cold Spring Harbor.
5. J.D. Watson. 1968. *The double helix: A personal account of the discovery of the structure of DNA,* p. 7. Atheneum Press, New York.
6. J.D. Watson. "Manners," draft manuscript. 2001, 2002. The James D. Watson Collection, Cold Spring Harbor Laboratory Archives.
7. J.D. Watson. "Manners," draft manuscript. 2001, 2002. The James D. Watson Collection, Cold Spring Harbor Laboratory Archives.
8. J.D. Watson. 2000. Bragg's Foreword to *The double helix.* In *A passion for DNA: Genes, genomes, and society,* p. 33. Cold Spring Harbor Laboratory Press, Cold Spring Harbor, New York.
9. J.D. Watson. 2000. *A passion for DNA: Genes, genomes, and society,* p. 36. Cold Spring Harbor Laboratory Press, Cold Spring Harbor, New York.
10. J.D. Watson. "Manners," draft manuscript. 2001, 2002. The James D. Watson Collection, Cold Spring Harbor Laboratory Archives.
11. Francis Crick, letter to J.D. Watson, September 27, 1966. The James D. Watson Collection, Cold Spring Harbor Laboratory Archives.
12. J.D. Watson, letter to Francis Crick, September 29, 1966. The James D. Watson Collection, Cold Spring Harbor Laboratory Archives.
13. J.D. Watson, letter to Francis Crick, October 19, 1966. The James D. Watson Collection, Cold Spring Harbor Laboratory Archives.
14. George Klein, letter to J.D. Watson, February 24, 1967. The James D. Watson Collection Cold Spring Harbor Laboratory Archives.
15. J.D. Bernal, letter to John Kendrew, December 20, 1966. The James D. Watson Collection, Cold Spring Harbor Laboratory Archives.
16. John Maddox, letter to J.D. Watson, April 13, 1967. The James D. Watson Collection, Cold Spring Harbor Laboratory Archives.
17. J.D. Watson, "Manners," draft manuscript. 2001, 2002. The James D. Watson Collection, Cold Spring Harbor Laboratory Archives.
18. Linus Pauling, letter to J.D. Watson, October 20, 1966. The James D. Watson Collection, Cold Spring Harbor Laboratory Archives.
19. J.D. Watson, letter to Nicolas Thompson, November 10, 1966. The James D. Watson Collection, Cold Spring Harbor Laboratory Archives.
20. J.D. Watson. 1968. Epilogue. In *The double helix: A personal account of the discovery of the structure of DNA,* p. 224. Atheneum Press, New York.
21. B. Maddox. 2002. *Rosalind Franklin: The dark lady of DNA.* HarperCollins, New York.
22. A conversation with James D. Watson. *Sci. Am.* April, pp. 66–69. Vol. 288(4).
23. J.D. Watson, letter to Sir Lawrence Bragg, July 25, 1967. The James D. Watson Collection, Cold Spring Harbor Laboratory Archives.
24. Francis Crick, letter to J.D. Watson, April 13, 1967. The James D. Watson Collection, Cold Spring Harbor Laboratory Archives.
25. Francis Crick, letter to J.D. Watson, April 13, 1967. The James D. Watson Collection, Cold Spring Harbor Laboratory Archives.
26. Francis Crick, letter to J.D. Watson, April 13, 1967. The James D. Watson Collection, Cold Spring Harbor Laboratory Archives.

27. W. Sullivan. 1968. A book that couldn't go to Harvard. *The New York Times,* February 15, pp. 1, 4.

28. Joyce Leibowitz, letter to J.D. Watson, May 25, 1967. The James D. Watson Collection, Cold Spring Harbor Laboratory Archives.

29. Alan Schwartz, letter to J.D. Watson, June 1, 1967. The James D. Watson Collection, Cold Spring Harbor Laboratory Archives.

30. Alan Schwartz, letter to J.D. Watson, June 1, 1967. The James D. Watson Collection, Cold Spring Harbor Laboratory Archives.

31. J.D. Watson. 1968. *The double helix: A personal account of the discovery of the structure of DNA.* Weidenfeld and Nicholson, London.

32. Dust jacket, *The Double Helix.* The James D. Watson Collection, Cold Spring Harbor Laboratory Archives.

33. J.D. Watson, cablegram to Weidenfeld and Nicholson, April 8, 1968. The James D. Watson Collection, Cold Spring Harbor Laboratory Archives.

34. J.D. Watson. [1968] 1980. *The double helix: A personal account of the discovery of the structure of DNA, A Norton critical edition* (ed. G.S. Stent). W.W. Norton, New York. Thirteen of these reviews are reprinted in the Norton Critical Edition of *The Double Helix.* This thoughtful compilation also includes the complete text of *The Double Helix* as well as retrospective views from Francis Crick, Linus Pauling, and Rosalind Franklin's last student, Aaron Klug. Background materials include reproductions of the original scientific papers in which the double helical structure of DNA was first presented in 1953 and 1954. Stent's own contribution, called "A Review of the Reviews," is an incisive analysis of the published reviews.

35. J.D. Watson. [1968] 1980. *The double helix: A personal account of the discovery of the structure of DNA, A Norton critical edition* (ed. G.S. Stent). W.W Norton, New York.

36. P.B. Medawar. 1968, Lucky Jim. *The New York Review of Books,* Vol. 10, no. 6, March 28.

37. R. Olby. 1974. *The path to the double helix.* The University of Washington Press, Seattle.

38. J.D. Watson, letter to Robert Olby, February 5, 1974. The James D. Watson Collection, Cold Spring Harbor Laboratory Archives.

39. J.D. Watson, letter to Robert Olby, February 5, 1974. The James D. Watson Collection, Cold Spring Harbor Laboratory Archives.

40. F. Crick. 1974. Foreword. In *The path to the double helix* (ed. R. Olby), p. v. The University of Washington Press, Seattle.

41. F. Crick. 1988. In *What mad pursuit: A personal view of scientific discovery,* p. 80. Basic Books, New York.

42. J.D. Watson, letter to Miss Cecelia McCarton, August 5, 1968. The James D. Watson Collection, Cold Spring Harbor Laboratory Archives.

43. J.D. Watson, letter to Miss Wendy Coates, April 7, 1977. The James D. Watson Collection, Cold Spring Harbor Laboratory Archives.

44. S. Jones. 1999. Introduction. In *The double helix: A personal account of the discovery of the structure of DNA.* Penguin Books, London.

GENES, GIRLS, AND GAMOW

"The story starts when I was an unmarried 25-year-old and thought more about girls than genes. It is as much a tale of love as of ideas." JDW, PREFACE, P. XII, *GGG*

More than a decade after the publication of *The Double Helix*, Watson started writing a second memoir of his early years, initially entitled "A Good Fortune—A History of a Science Episode Immersed in a Love Story."[1] But the writing was frequently interrupted by his professional responsibilities and obligations. He wrote a few chapters in London in 1986 and the Prologue in 1991. Watson hoped to complete the book while he was a visiting professor in Oxford in 1994, but found it difficult because his recall of events was unsatisfactory.

"I found an almost diary-like description of the people entering my life as well as my scientific brainstorms of the moment." JDW, PREFACE, *GGG*

But then he received an unexpected *aide-mémoire*. Watson had become acquainted with the family of the Harvard evolutionary biologist Ernst Mayr during the summers spent at Cold Spring Harbor Laboratory in the late 1940s when he was a young graduate student.

The Morning After

A GOOD FORTUNE

A history of science episode immersed in a love story

trying to keep the party going after the double helix

J. D. Watson

Copyright 1999 by J.D. Watson
Not to be reprinted without permission

Title page of an earlier version of the manuscript of *Genes, Girls, and Gamow*. The title, in 1997, was "A Good Fortune: A history of science episode immersed in a love story," and it was probably intended to echo the first sentence of Jane Austen's *Pride and Prejudice*, which is quoted at the beginning of the book: "It is a truth universally acknowledged, that a single man in possession of a good fortune, must be in want of a wife." This 1999 editing of the title page shows that Watson was still searching for a suitable title. (Courtesy of the James D. Watson Collection, Cold Spring Harbor Laboratory Archives.)

In 1953, during a summer highlighted by his formal presentation of the double helix to the scientists assembled at Cold Spring Harbor for the annual Symposium, Watson fell in love with Mayr's daughter, Christa, a young woman about to enter college. During the subse-

THE girl I was in love with had gone off to Europe
for a year abroad and I knew I would follow her. But I
was afraid this might be a mistake, for American girls,
of the type I usually fall for, have to get the Continent
out of their systems and the quickest way to let this
happen is to leave them alone. Thus I let her board the
ship by herself and some weeks later I flew to London. Almost immediately I went up to Cambridge to
see the Cricks and to joke again with Peter Pauling. It
was then the summer of 1955 and he was living out of
college, sharing a flat with his sister Linda. She had
recently come over from the States to look after him,
hoping conceivably that sisterly advice would help
him choose a sensible wife from among the numerous
"popsies" who were floating into his life.

Following a fortnight of parties on the "backs," I
had to get closer to the girl and went over to Paris for
a couple of days before ending up in Switzerland.
There I had a month to wait until at her uncle's home
I was to see her blond hair. And, as doing nothing
would have made me thoroughly incapable of appear-
ing unnervous when I finally said hello, I arranged to
join some friends who were going into the Alps.

Just before I left Cambridge, Alfred Tissieres, then
a Fellow at King's, had said he would get me to the

Typeset Galley 1 of *The Double Helix* (1968). The correction shows the deletion of the first two paragraphs of the opening page, which refer to the pursuit of "the girl I was in love with" and to Peter and Linda Pauling. Apparently too much of a digression from the double helix story, these characters reappear as central to the *Genes, Girls, and Gamow* story published more than 30 years later. (Courtesy of the James D. Watson Collection, Cold Spring Harbor Laboratory Archives.)

quent three years, Watson wrote about 60 letters to Christa, expressing his affection and commenting on his life and opinions. A reference to this relationship was initially part of the Prologue to *The Double Helix*, which begins

ATHENAEUM

551 South Hill Avenue, Pasadena 5, California

Tuesday Evening

Dear Christa

The last two days have been rather a waste of time. On both days I have been afflicted with visitors, and todays were the worst, since I had to dine with them and spend most of the evening with the usual small talk about the history of caltech, the advantages of campus

CLARE COLLEGE CAMBRIDGE

September 2, 1953

Dear Christa

Your last letter arrived a day after I left for the continent and the Swiss Alps. I returned to Cambridge two days ago but have already left (I am writing fr____

to embark early tomorrow morning for N_

by the Georgic, an old and slow boat w___

which in the winter takes troops to Au____

advantage of being one class and so ___

be possible to talk with anyone.

Our practical joke succeeded

completely, fell for the Honorary Professorship.

wrote an acceptance to Pauling. There are very many answers

which I should like to write now but cannot because of

lack of time. However when I return to the states, I shall completely

Watson's letters to Christa Mayr written from The Athenaeum at the California Institute of Technology in Pasadena, California and from Clare College, Cambridge University. Christa saved his letters from the 1950s and offered to return them to him years later. They contained many details of daily thoughts and activities, details that were useful in writing *Genes, Girls, and Gamow*. (*Inset*) Christa Mayr in Cambridge, Massachusetts, 1954. This photograph appears in Chapter 3 of *Genes, Girls, and Gamow*. (Courtesy of the James D. Watson Collection, Cold Spring Harbor Laboratory Archives. Reprinted with permission from Christa Mayr Menzel.)

The girl I was in love with had gone off to Europe for a year abroad and I knew I would follow her.[2]

This reference was subsequently deleted in the book's galley proofs.[3]

Forty years later, in 1995, he received a letter from Christa Mayr Menzel offering to return all his earlier correspondence with her. When Watson received the letters, he discovered all sorts of details, making it possible for him to finish writing the book. His correspondence with his parents during his stay in Cambridge had provided material for *The Double Helix*. But later, because he was writing primarily to Christa, letters to his parents were much less detailed.[4]

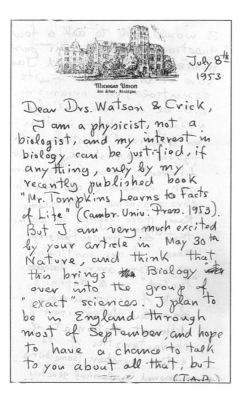

First page of letter from George Gamow, July 8, 1953, introducing himself to Watson and Crick and writing of his excitement over their article in the May 30th issue of *Nature*: "[I] think that this brings Biology over into the group of 'exact' sciences." This and other letters and notes from Gamow are reprinted in the back of *Genes, Girls, and Gamow*. (Courtesy of the James D. Watson Collection, Cold Spring Harbor Laboratory Archives. Reprinted with permission from Elfriede Gamow, Ph.D.)

"This story . . . has Geo Gamow to keep us on our toes." JDW,
PREFACE, *GGG*

Watson had another cache of letters from the 1953–1956 period
that he thought had book potential. These were from George Gamow,
who was credited with seminal contributions to the "Big Bang" theory of the origin of the universe. Gamow had no formal training as a
biologist, but after encountering Watson and Crick's second *Nature*
paper published soon after the announcement of the double helix, he
was struck by the mathematical implications of a code embodied in the
millions of iterations of the four DNA bases A, C, T, and G. He is said
to have read the entire *Nature* paper while standing at the mailbox
where he retrieved his weekly copy of the journal.[5]

Gamow introduced himself to Watson and Crick with a zany
handwritten note, beginning an association that led to the foundation
of the RNA Tie Club. The Club consisted of 20 prominent scientists,

George Gamow (*right*) joking with Alex Rich (*left*) at the 1963 Symposium at Cold Spring Harbor. Gamow's maverick personality intrigued the young Watson. More importantly, his notions
of a genetic code in DNA, though incorrect, prompted Watson and others to think more deeply
about the problem. (Courtesy of the Cold Spring Harbor Laboratory Archives.)

(*Left*) The RNA tie designed by George Gamow and worn by members of the "RNA Tie Club." The tie depicts a stylized single-stranded RNA chain. The colors of the original RNA tie were chartreuse and yellow on a black background. Watson arranged for the tie to be manufactured by a haberdasher in Los Angeles.

Rnatie Club

"Do or die, or don't try"

OFFICERS
GEO GAMOW · SYNTHESIZER
GEORGE WASHINGTON UNIVERSITY
JIM WATSON · OPTIMIST
HARVARD UNIVERSITY
FRANCIS CRICK · PESSIMIST
CAMBRIDGE UNIVERSITY
MARTINAS YCAS · ARCHIVIST
QUARTERMASTER R. & D. LABS.
ALEX RICH · LORD PRIVY SEAL
NAT. INST. MENTAL HEALTH

July 4, 1955

Dear Pro,

This is the first official club circular.

First, the assignments of tie pins (which, as you know, were randomized):

1) ALA - G. Gamow
2) ARG - A. Rich
3) ASP - P. Doty
4) ASN - R. Ledley
5) CYS - M. Ycas
6) GLU - R. Williams
7) GLN - A. Dounce
8) GLY - R. Feynman
9) HIS - M. Calvin
10) ISO - N. Simons
11) LEU - E. Teller
12) LYS - E. Chargaff
13) MET - N. Metropolis
14) PHE - G. Stent
15) PRO - J. Watson
16) SER - H. Gordon
17) THR - L. Orgel
18) TRY - M. Delbrück
19) TYR - F. Crick
20) VAL - S. Brenner

From this list, 13 members have obtained their tie pins while the remaining 7 are still stubbornly holding out.

For RNA ties, please write to Jim Watson at *Cambridge* University.

The first matter of business is the election of honorary base members. The organization committee proposes two candidates out of the maximum possible number of four:

1) Dr. Fritz Lipmann for: CY
2) Dr. Albert Szent-Gyorgyi for: AD

(These assignments of bases were made by random choice).

Each of the 20 members of the club is welcome to send his vote for both of these two candidates.

For a positive vote: include $1.00 for each candidate (if only $1.00 is included, please specify for which of the two candidates you are voting)

(*Above*) "Rnatie Club" letterhead printed with motto, "Do or die, or don't try" and the list of officers. The purchase and distribution of ties and individual tiepins and the election of honorary members were the subjects of "the first official club circular" sent out by Gamow. (Courtesy of the James D. Watson Collection, Cold Spring Harbor Laboratory Archives.)

each named for a particular amino acid. It had its own stationery and a special tie emblazoned with a schematic RNA chain. Members shared preprints of their work in the spirit of communication that characterized this period in molecular biology. Gamow's letters and his practical jokes intrigued Watson:

> *For years I have wanted to write about how the RNA Tie Club came into existence, inserting Geo's oft-illustrated, wacky letters into the intellectual climate that surrounded the spiritual upheaval among biologists after the discovery of the double helix.*[6]

Some of Gamow's letters are reproduced in *Genes, Girls, and Gamow*. Watson explained that "I think my chief reason for wanting to write this book was Gamow's letters."[7]

"...I try to capture the spirit of my youth and purposely do not make reflective judgment on where I was going right or wrong."
JDW, Preface, *GGG*

The manuscript that became the memoir *Genes, Girls and Gamow* describes the three and a half year period between the discovery of the DNA structure in the spring of 1953 and the beginning of Watson's career as a professor at Harvard University in the fall of 1956. It has three themes: Watson's scientific pursuits, his preoccupation with finding a girlfriend (and maybe even a wife), and his relationship with Gamow. Watson himself describes it as a story about Americans in Cambridge: "Myself and Linda Pauling and Peter Pauling [daughter and son of Linus Pauling], all trying to find something more interesting than America in England. And none of us doing so very well!"[8]

Some who read drafts of the manuscript found it too revealing; others declared it uninteresting. Neil Patterson, who published Watson's first book, *The Molecular Biology of the Gene*, in 1965, stayed up all night reading it and in the morning told Watson that, though he liked it a lot, it needed stylistic changes.[9] Others advised Watson against publication. Watson rejected such advice: "Once you write the book you publish it. I didn't write it to put in a vault."[10] Besides, "others will get it wrong," he once commented, when discussing some of the reasons for writing his own memoirs.[11]

After reading six or seven chapters during a visit to Cold Spring Harbor, Michael Rodgers of Oxford University Press told Watson that he thought the manuscript very publishable.[12] He received the completed manuscript in the spring of 2000 and found it ". . . charming, amusing, in places gripping, in places touching, and throughout deeply interesting."[13] Rodgers felt it was "an important record of how things actually were in those heroic days," and the Mayr letters gave the story freshness, authenticity, and immediacy.[14] In the United States, the manuscript reached George Andreou, editor for A.A. Knopf, who liked it, too. Andreou and Rodgers persuaded Watson that a section called "Cast of Characters" was necessary so readers could keep track of the large number of characters in Watson's story and that

Peter Pauling (*left*) and Watson (*right*) at Harvard (ca. 1966), ten years after the period described in *Genes, Girls, and Gamow*. (Courtesy Harvard University Archives. Photo credit: Rick Stafford.) Watson asked Peter Pauling to write the Foreword to the book. In it Pauling noted that many people "will be unhappy with the book (the Victims). Without them, however, there would be no book." He concludes, "As unappointed leader of the Victims, I hope they [the readers] will forgive or at least be lenient with both me and Jim."

each chapter should have a dateline to help the reader remember where and when events were occurring.[15]

The book also needed a Foreword and Watson was very keen to have Peter Pauling write this, for the same reason he had proposed that Lawrence Bragg write the Foreword for *The Double Helix*. Pauling and Watson had frequented the same social set in Cambridge, but Pauling endured difficult circumstances in the mid-1950s, as the manuscript describes. His agreement was uncertain, but eventually he consented and wrote an eccentric but entirely appropriate piece that was published essentially unchanged.[16] (Peter Pauling died in 2002.)

The original manuscript had ended with Watson walking in Harvard Square, forlorn and sad. But Andreou and Rodgers proposed that the book end with Watson's happy and enduring marriage to Elizabeth Lewis in 1968.[17, 18]

The final title chosen for this second memoir was *Genes, Girls, and Gamow: After The Double Helix*. In the Preface, Watson points out that the book recounts "the personal agonies that for many of us dimmed the glamour of the double helix's first glory days."[19] It was a book about failure, in relationships and in scientific ambitions.[20] He also pointed out that he was portraying himself as "the inexperienced and more self-centered person I once was."[21]

Michael Rodgers, Oxford University Press, who worked with George Andreou of A.A. Knopf to persuade Watson to add the "Cast of Characters" at the beginning, the datelines for each chapter, and the Epilogue at the end. (Photo courtesy Michael Rodgers.)

Newlyweds Elizabeth Lewis and James Watson, 1968. (Courtesy of the James D. Watson Collection, Cold Spring Harbor Laboratory Archives.) The Epilogue to *Genes, Girls, and Gamow* brings events up to 1968 and Watson's marriage to Elizabeth Lewis, ending the narrative on a happy note: "Now, more than thirty years later, she remains very much a sweet peach."

"There will be other readers . . . who nonetheless feel that many of the personal facts I write below are not worth being passed on to the future." JDW, Preface, *GGG*

Oxford University Press published *Genes, Girls and Gamow* in the United Kingdom in late 2001 and a few months later the United States edition was released by A.A. Knopf. It was widely reviewed, more frequently in newspapers and magazines than *The Double Helix* had been.

The science writer Matt Ridley commented

Jim and Liz Watson in 1991 in front of the Beckman Neuroscience Building at Cold Spring Harbor Laboratory, where Watson has his office. (Courtesy of the James D. Watson Collection, Cold Spring Harbor Laboratory Archives.)

Genes, Girls, and Gamow . . . *broke new ground . . . abandoning smooth prose to tell a scientific saga with the clumsy style and hesitant uncertainty of a young man's mind. Had it been a novel, it would have been praised for its post-modern, innovatory syntax. But once again the world was not ready for Watson, and many literary-minded reviewers gave him no quarter.*[22]

Many critics in Britain failed to find redeeming qualities in the work. The *New Statesman* referred to it as "bloated,"[23] and *The Spectator* as "the diary of a compulsive ogler, constantly thwarted."[24] In contrast, *The Boston Globe* found that the book gave "a fuller demonstration of what it is that allowed so young and inexperienced a man—inexperienced in science as well as life—to make such a landmark discovery,"[25] and noted that Watson was looking for a wife: "It wasn't about lust; it was romance."[26]

Some female reviewers were decidedly critical. Barbara Ehrenreich, writing for *The New York Times*, took particular offense at Watson's use of the diminutive form "girl" when referring to women, and to other hints of sexual discrimination, even though Watson was writing about a period almost 50 years ago.[27] And *The Harvard Crimson's* reviewer took exception to Watson's sexual pomposity, such as in his reference to "finding" his wife.[28]

Rodgers and Andreou were disappointed, but not dismayed, by the reviews. Rodgers felt that many reviewers simply did not get it, expecting this book to be another double helix story.[29] Rodgers pointed out that ". . . there's only one double helix story—and you can't cap that."[30] For Andreou, the book was clearly "a pendant to a greater body of work," not deserving of the ungenerous way some had treated it.[31] "It's perhaps not everyone's cup of tea," he said, "but the justification of publishing it as an historical document is quite obvious."[32]

The American historian of science Horace Freeland Judson, reviewing the book for *Nature*, expressed surprise that the book had been published at all and questioned Watson's scientific ethics in "arrogating chief credit for [the discovery of] messenger RNA to work he

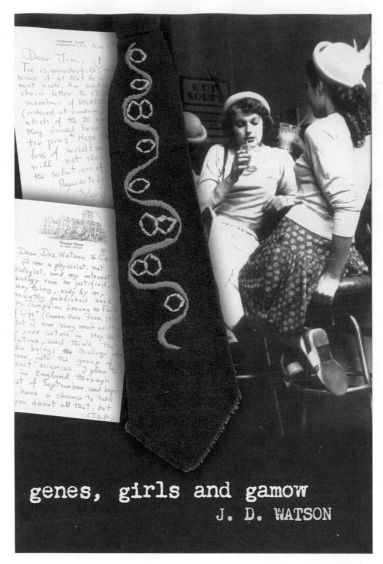

Genes, Girls and Gamow was originally published in Great Britain by Oxford University Press, London, in 2001. The dust jacket of the hardcover edition shows the famous RNA tie, handwritten letters by Watson, and a vintage photograph. (Reproduced by permission of Oxford University Press.)

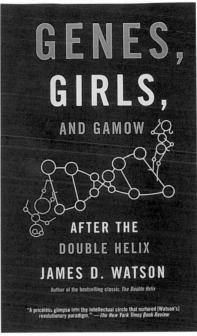

A.A. Knopf, New York, published the hardcover edition of *Genes, Girls, and Gamow* in 2002 in the United States. Since then, a paperback edition has been issued by Vintage (2003). Both U.S. editions are shown here. (Reproduced courtesy of A.A. Knopf and Vintage.)

did at Harvard,"[33] an accusation that prompted an apology to Watson from *Nature*. A more balanced review in *New Scientist* noted that the book "shows the perils of hitting the scientific jackpot before you're quite ready to grow up. Behind all the jollity, all the travelling, drinking and dining (there's a meal or party every five pages or so), lies a lot of unhappiness."[34]

In *Genes, Girls, and Gamow*, Watson again attempted what may be considered a unique literary format for a scientist—a mixture of frank memoir, real science and its execution, and a portrait of an icon of the time (Gamow). Opinions vary on how successful he was.

Notes

1. Interview with J.D. Watson, March 12, 2003.
2. J.D. Watson. "Honest Jim." Draft manuscript. James D. Watson Archive, Harvard University.
3. Galley proof of *The Double Helix*. The James D. Watson Collection, Cold Spring Harbor Laboratory Archives.
4. Interview with J.D. Watson, March 12, 2003.
5. Marshall Nirenberg, Lecture at CSHL, March 1, 2003.
6. J.D. Watson. Preface. 2002. In *Genes, girls, and Gamow: After the double helix*, p. xi. A.A. Knopf, New York.
7. Interview with J.D. Watson, February 9, 2002, Cold Spring Harbor.
8. Interview with J.D. Watson, February 9, 2002, Cold Spring Harbor.
9. Interview with Neil Patterson, March 17, 2003.
10. Interview with J.D. Watson, March 12, 2003.
11. J.D. Watson, personal communication.
12. Interview with Michael Rodgers, March 24, 2003.
13. Michael Rodgers, e-mail to James Watson, June 27, 2000.
14. Interview with Michael Rodgers, March 24, 2003.
15. Interview with Michael Rodgers, March 24, 2003.
16. Interview with Michael Rodgers, March 24, 2003.
17. Interview with George Andreou, April 4, 2003.
18. Interview with Michael Rodgers, March 24, 2003.
19. J.D. Watson. 2002. Epilogue. In *Genes, girls, and Gamow: After the double helix*, p. 236. A.A. Knopf, New York.
20. Interview with J.D. Watson, February 9, 2002, Cold Spring Harbor.
21. J.D. Watson. 2002. Preface. In *Genes, girls, and Gamow: After the double helix*, p. xii. A.A. Knopf, New York.
22. M. Ridley. 2003. Foreword. In *Inspiring science, Jim Watson and the age of DNA*, p. xvii. Cold Spring Harbor Laboratory Press, Cold Spring Harbor, New York.
23. Michael Barrett. 2002. From double helix to double cross. *New Statesman*, January 7.
24. N. Fearn. 2001. The bonding of base pairs. *The Spectator*, December 29.
25. M. Feeney. 2002. Romancing the molecule. *The Boston Globe*, February 27.
26. M. Feeney. 2002. Romancing the molecule. *The Boston Globe*, February 27.
27. B. Ehrenreich. 2002. Double helix, single guy. *New York Times Review of Books*, February 24.
28. A.W. Lai. 2002. Unzipping Watson's Helix. *The Harvard Crimson*, February 22.
29. Interview with Michael Rodgers, March 24, 2003.
30. Interview with Michael Rodgers, March 24, 2003.
31. Interview with George Andreou, April 4, 2003.
32. Interview with George Andreou, April 4, 2003.
33. H.F. Judson. 2001. Honest Jim: The sequel. *Nature* **413:** 775.
34. R. Bridgman. 2001. Songs of innocence and experience. *New Scientist*, November 24, p. 42.

ADVOCACY

THE DNA STORY,
DIRECTOR'S REPORTS,
AND OTHER ESSAYS

"Our first reaction was one of pure joy . . ." JDW/JT, PROLOGUE, *DNA STORY*, P. VII

In the early 1970s, methods were invented that allowed DNA molecules from different sources to be combined in the laboratory. The result was called recombinant DNA, and it led to a period of considerable apprehension and controversy in both the scientific and public communities. To document this revolution in science and the scientific and public reaction to it (subsequently referred to as the "recombinant DNA controversy"), Watson and his coauthor John Tooze assembled materials for a book called *The DNA Story: A Documentary History of Gene Cloning*, published by W.H. Freeman in 1981. The work featured an innovative style and format in which the assorted documents, speeches, letters, and photographs spoke for themselves in this passionate and sometimes bitter debate. To understand the book itself, it is useful to briefly consider recombinant DNA techniques and the issues they raised when they first emerged.

*". . . by April 1974 we did not think recombinant DNA could be
kept under the rug. . ."* JDW/JT, PROLOGUE, *DNA STORY*

In the early 1970s, a dialogue began among scientists about the
possible consequences of "genetic engineering"—altering an organism's genetic constitution. In response to a sense of disquiet, Paul Berg
of Stanford University, a pioneer of gene cloning and future Nobel
Laureate, organized a gathering of prominent molecular biologists in
January 1973 at a conference center in Asilomar State Park near San
Francisco, California, to discuss some of the issues.

Unease among molecular biologists persisted. At a Gordon Research Conference six months later, a narrow vote was taken by a

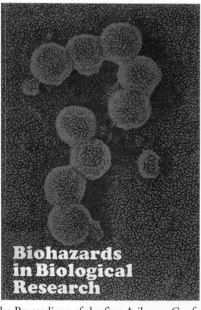

The Proceedings of the first Asilomar Conference, held in Pacific Grove, California in January 1973, were published by Cold Spring Harbor Laboratory in a book entitled *Biohazards in Biological Research*. The volume was edited by A. Hellman, M.N. Oxman, and R. Pollack. In the Preface they note: "With widespread interest and growing participation of many laboratories in the problems of animal cell biology and tumor viruses, there is a growing need for consideration of potential health hazards. Much of the experience and knowledge concerning such hazard, imaginary as well as real, is known to only a few people and is not widely publicized."

minority of the conference participants to draft a letter to the U.S. National Academy of Sciences and the journal *Science* to express concern about possible risks associated with the unregulated manipulation of DNA. They called for the establishment of "a study committee to consider this problem and to recommend specific actions or guidelines should that seem appropriate."[1]

In response to these suggestions, the National Academy of Sciences established a blue-ribbon committee, chaired by Paul Berg, which issued a letter signed by all ten members. The letter, published in both *Science* and *Nature,* suggested a possible moratorium on recombinant DNA research. Watson attended the first Asilomar conference and was among the ten signatories to the moratorium letter. The letter generated intense interest from the media and, motivated by the quickening momentum of events, Berg and others convened a second meeting, Asilomar II, in February 1975.

"I don't know of a single person who does recombinant DNA who feels the tiniest apprehension." JDW, *PASSION FOR DNA*, P. 57

Watson was one of many scientists who initially saw no harm in convening Asilomar II, or in calling for some scientific restraint, especially in the post-Watergate atmosphere of self-confession.[2] But on reflecting more deeply, he concluded that merely holding the conference attended by the leadership of the DNA world and open to the press would imply that the scientific community itself was alarmed about its own work at some level. He wrote in the Cold Spring Harbor Laboratory Annual Report for 1976,

> *The very act of setting up committees to pinpoint the "most risky" experiments could only magnify the public fear that we biologists now had our own diabolic form of the bomb.*[3]

Watson asked why all clear-thinking scientists had failed to recognize the risk of publicly debating the dangers of recombinant DNA research when they had been working with highly pathogenic organisms and other noxious agents for decades without public concern.

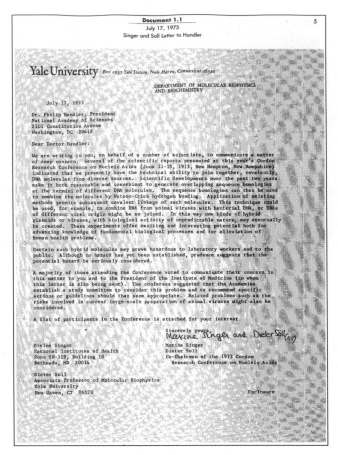

July 17, 1973, letter from Maxine Singer and Dieter Soll to Dr. Philip Handler, President of the National Academy of Sciences. They note, of the new recombinant DNA technology, "These experiments offer exciting and interesting potential both for advancing knowledge of fundamental biological processes and for alleviation of human health problems. Certain such hybrid molecules may prove hazardous to laboratory workers and to the public. Although no hazard has yet been established, prudence suggests that the potential hazard be seriously considered." Singer and Soll further suggested the establishment of a study committee to consider the problem, which the National Academy subsequently did, appointing Paul Berg as Chairman. (Reprinted from *The DNA Story*. Courtesy of Maxine Singer.)

And why recommend guidelines of any sort? He sought answers in the social and political climate of the time:

Watergate was still with us and the national mood was very much to come clean with what one was up to. . . . Unfortunately, none

Left to right: Maxine Singer, Norton Zinder, Sidney Brenner, and Paul Berg at the second Asilomar Conference, 1975. (Courtesy of the Cold Spring Harbor Laboratory Archives.) Because of the presence of the press the public became concerned over the potential hazards of recombinant DNA research. In particular, *Rolling Stone*, June 19, 1975 (p. 36) provided extensive coverage in an article entitled "The Pandora's Box Congress: 140 Scientists Ask: Now that We Can Rewrite the Genetic Code, What Are We Going to Say?" written by Michael Rogers. (The reporter Michael Rogers is not to be confused with Michael Rodgers of Oxford University Press, who published *Genes, Girls and Gamow.*)

> *of us seriously questioned whether we might be alerting the public unnecessarily and by doing so give recombinant DNA doomsday scenarios a credibility they didn't deserve. . . . The minute the moratorium was announced, we had, in effect, asked the public to join us in the decision-making process. . . . Why would we have actually halted our experiments if we weren't really worried?*[4]

Thus, the dawning of the recombinant DNA era was an irksome one for scientists and a costly one for U.S. taxpayers. Formal guidelines were promulgated by the National Institutes of Health (NIH) in 1976 (although not written into federal law) and penalties were imposed for their violation. However, eventual recognition of the huge potential and apparent safety of recombinant DNA technology by the late 1970s resulted in the abandonment of restrictions, except for experiments with highly virulent organisms.

James Watson (*left*) and Sidney Brenner (*right*) at the Asilomar Conference, California, 1975. (Courtesy of the Cold Spring Harbor Laboratory Archives.) Watson grew to feel that the mere holding of the meeting, and the subsequent publicity, might unduly alarm the public.

"It [recombinant DNA] is an obligatory fact of life." JDW, *PASSION FOR DNA*, P. 56

By 1980, there was a story to tell. It had begun with calls for a worldwide moratorium on recombinant DNA and culminated almost eight years later in a worldwide boom industry based on DNA.[5] Watson had the idea of telling the story in documentary form, as a kind of scrapbook,[6] incorporating original documents, photographs, and articles. *The DNA Story* became the second publishing collaboration between Watson and Neil Patterson, by then President of W.H. Freeman. Patterson argued that the book was a good way to present the various points of view to the world and to demonstrate the shrill character of journalistic effort toward closing things down or constraining them.[7]

Neil Patterson (ca. 1981). (Photo courtesy of Neil Patterson.) *The DNA Story* was the second publishing collaboration between Watson and Neil Patterson. Watson and Tooze originally signed the book with W.W. Norton, while Patterson was Director of the College Department. However, when he was appointed President of W.H. Freemen in 1981, he naturally wanted to take the book with him. A February 11, 1980 letter from Norton expresses disappointment that Norton would not be publishing the book, but that "we entirely respect, even honor, your reasons for going with Neil."

John Tooze, Executive Secretary to the European Molecular Biology Organization (EMBO) in Heidelberg, Germany, was recruited as coauthor. Tooze, an experienced editor, found that because Watson was a meticulous collector of documents and correspondence, most of the material needed for the book was already available.[8]

The book consisted of 16 chapters that guided the reader chronologically from the Gordon Research Conference in June 1973 to the public stock offering by the embryonic biotechnology company Genentech in September 1980. Each chapter had a very brief introduction to guide the reader from one section to another (the authors had decided to avoid voicing their own opinions regarding the events portrayed and to let the documents and position papers speak for themselves).[9] To portray for the general reader the science that provided the necessary background to the controversy, Watson and Tooze enlisted the talented freelance scientific illustrator George Kelvin to produce a graphic section at the beginning of the book called "Visualizing DNA."

John Tooze (*left*) and James Watson (*right*), 1981. (Courtesy of the Cold Spring Harbor Laboratory Archives. Photo credit: Fred Weiss.) At the time, Tooze was head of the European Molecular Biology Organization (EMBO) and Watson was Director of the Cold Spring Harbor Laboratory. In the Prologue they wrote: "We personally believe that recombinant DNA research is best left virtually unregulated." However, they decided that, in putting together the book, they would let the various positions and documents stand on their own merits. More than 20 years later, the collected primary source documents continue to tell the story with immediacy and freshness.

Watson and Tooze concluded *The DNA Story* with a 55-page section on genetics and molecular biology that described the basic techniques of recombining DNA and of identifying cloned genes, and what had been learned by using the techniques.[10] The authors' purpose in including this section was to demonstrate that

> *recombinant DNA was no ordinary scientific advance. Once available the academic community seized upon it as a way of overcoming obstacles in the advance of molecular genetics.[11]*

The DNA Story: A Documentary History of Gene Cloning was published in 1981 by W.H. Freeman and dedicated to Francis Crick. A

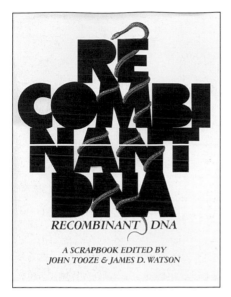

Evolution of the book cover. (*Left*) A proposed cover design for "Recombinant DNA, A Scrapbook edited by John Tooze & James D. Watson." (Courtesy of The James D. Watson Collection, Cold Spring Harbor Laboratory Archives.) Both the title and the image of the menacing snake were eventually abandoned. (*Right*) Final cover design for *The DNA Story* with a double helix coiled into a question mark. Some of the issues raised by the recombinant DNA controversy are still unresolved, and are echoed by similar ethical and political issues today. (Reproduced with permission from W.H. Freeman.)

picture of a smiling Crick wearing his RNA tie appears opposite the Prologue and the dedication on the Acknowledgments page reads, "We dedicate this book to Francis Crick." It was widely reviewed. Some critics were pleased by its historic value; others would have preferred a more conventional format. Yet others wanted to know about gene cloning, not about its politics. *The San Diego Union* commented that it was a "book in which almost anyone can browse and find something of interest—whether for knowledge, aesthetics or entertainment."[12] But H.J. Geiger, in *Science '81*, called it "a disaster [that] almost defies attempts to read it through," concluding that "drawing on the raw materials of the controversy by summarizing it, interpreting it, and

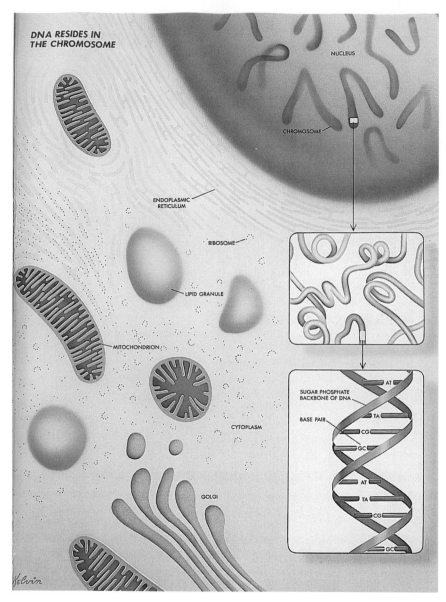

Visualizing DNA. This eight-page, four-color section appeared in the beginning of *The DNA Story*. It was drawn by the talented artist George Kelvin and provided a "technicolor preview" to the book. The authors write in the preface, "We and our publisher came to realize that the essence of the techniques of recombinant DNA might best be conveyed to those not interested in scientific details in a pictorial manner." (Reproduced with permission from W.H. Freeman.)

Francis Crick, 1956. The Acknowledgments page of *The DNA Story* notes: "We dedicate this book to Francis Crick." He is shown here wearing the RNA Club tie. Watson also dedicated *DNA: The Secret of Life*, published in 2003, to Crick, the only person he honored by two book dedications. (Reproduced with permission from W.H. Freeman. Photo credit: Francis DiGennaro.)

explaining it, Watson and Tooze have given us the raw materials themselves: almost 500 pages of documents alone, a sprawl of scientific reports, journal articles, newspaper and magazine reports, editorials, letters, records of congressional hearings, cartoons, even the backs of envelopes. . . .The book is sprawling, cluttered, wasteful, and disorganized. DNA deserves better."[13]

The *Philadelphia Inquirer* commented that

> *A number of important assumptions are presented as if they were incontestable, when in fact they are very much open to question.*[14]

But Gunther Stent, acknowledging that a deeper historical perspective would be needed, noted that we are "obliged to judge this episode in the here-and-now. And for trying to make an informed judgment, there can be no better help than the documents of this book."[15]

Pages from *The DNA Story* showing original documents, published articles, and newspaper headlines laid out like a scrapbook. (Reproduced with permission from W.H. Freeman.) (*Continued on the following pages.*)

". . . we shall have to spend more time educating the public." JDW,
DIRECTOR'S REPORT, 1976

During the period surveyed in *The DNA Story*, Watson wrote a number of articles on recombinant DNA for general periodicals and magazines, including *The New York Times*,[16] *The New Republic*,[17]

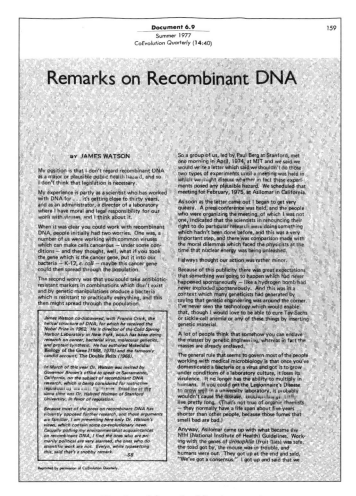

Document 6.9
Summer 1977
CoEvolution Quarterly (14:40)

159

Remarks on Recombinant DNA

BY JAMES WATSON

My position is that I don't regard recombinant DNA as a major or plausible public health hazard, and so I don't think that legislation is necessary.

My experience is partly as a scientist who has worked with DNA for . . . it's getting close to thirty years, and as an administrator, a director of a laboratory where I have moral and legal responsibility for our work with viruses, and I think about it.

When it was clear you could work with recombinant DNA, people initially had two worries. One was, a number of us were working with common viruses which can make cells cancerous — under some conditions — and they thought, well, what if you took the gene which is the cancer gene, put it into our bacteria — K-12, *e. coli* — maybe this cancer gene could then spread through the population.

The second worry was that you could take antibiotic-resistant markers in combinations which don't exist and by genetic manipulations produce a bacteria which is resistant to practically everything, and this then might spread through the population.

James Watson co-discovered, with Francis Crick, the helical structure of DNA, for which he received the Nobel Prize in 1962. He is director of the Cold Spring Harbor Laboratory in New York, which has been doing research on cancer, bacterial virus, molecular genetics, and protein synthesis. He has authored Molecular Biology of the Gene *(1968, 1970) and the famously candid account,* The Double Helix *(1968).*

In March of this year Dr. Watson was invited by Governor Brown's office to speak in Sacramento, California, on the subject of recombinant DNA research, which is being considered for restrictive legislation by the state. Testifying at the same time was Dr. Halsted Holman of Stanford University, in favor of regulation.

Because most of the press on recombinant DNA has violently opposed further research, and those arguments are familiar, I am presenting here only Dr. Watson's views, which contain some co-evolutionary news. Casually polling my environmentalist acquaintances on recombinant DNA, I find the ones who are primarily political are very alarmed, the ones who do scientific work are not. Evelyn, while typesetting this, said that's a snobby remark.   —SB

So a group of us, led by Paul Berg at Stanford, met one morning in April, 1974, at MIT and we said we would write a letter which said we shouldn't do those two types of experiments until a meeting was held in which we might discuss whether in fact these experiments posed any plausible hazard. We scheduled that meeting for February, 1975, at Asilomar in California.

As soon as the letter came out I began to get very queasy. A press conference was held, and the people who were organizing the meeting, of which I was not one, indicated that the scientists in renouncing their right to do particular research were doing something which hadn't been done before, and this was a very important step, and there was comparison made with the moral dilemmas which faced the physicists at the time that nuclear energy was being unleashed.

I always thought our action was rather minor.

Because of this publicity there was great expectations that something was going to happen which had never happened spontaneously — like a hydrogen bomb had never exploded spontaneously. And this was in a context which many geneticists had generated by saying that genetic engineering was around the corner. I've never seen the technology which would enable that, though I would love to be able to cure Tay-Sachs or sickle-cell anemia or any of these things by inserting genetic material.

A lot of people think that somehow you can enslave the masses by genetic engineering, whereas in fact the masses are already enslaved.

The general rule that seems to govern most of the people working with medical microbiology is that once you've domesticated a bacteria or a virus and got it to grow under conditions of a laboratory culture, it loses its virulence. It no longer has the ability to multiply in humans. If you could get the Legionnaire's Disease to grow well in a university laboratory, it probably wouldn't cause the disease. Unfortunately, they'll live pretty long. (That's not true of organic chemists — they normally have a life span about five years shorter than other people, because those fumes that smell bad are bad.)

Anyway, Asilomar came up with what became the NIH (National Institute of Health) Guidelines. Working with the genes of *drosophila* (fruit flies) was safe, the toad got by, the mouse was in trouble, and humans were out. They got up at the end and said, "We've got a consensus." I got up and said that we

Reprinted by permission of CoEvolution Quarterly.

(Continued from the following page.)

CoEvolution Quarterly,[18] *Time Magazine,*[19] *The Washington Post,*[20] and *Nature.*[21] He also used his Director's Reports in the *Cold Spring Harbor Laboratory Annual Report* to pursue his belief that it was essential that the general public be informed on this issue and understand the importance of basic research:

12

Document 1.6

July 18, 1974

Newspaper Headlines and Articles

The Washington Post, July 18, 1974

NAS Panel Warns of 'Hazards'

Halt in Genetic Work Urged

By Stuart Auerbach
Washington Post Staff Writer

A committee of the National Academy of Science fears that the new science of transferring genetic material from animals to bacteria could increase the incidence of cancer and could create drug-resistant strains of mutant germs that would cause new diseases.

In a report to be released today, the committee calls on scientists to postpone or abandon research in this field because of its "potential hazards," even though the research could benefit mankind.

The committee includes the researchers who developed during the past year new techniques that allow them to transfer bits of deoxyribonucleic acid (DNA) from ani-

mals or bacteria that contains genetic material into genetic material from bacteria.

This is the first time that scientists actively working in a field have called for voluntary restraints in their research, said Dr. Paul Berg of Stanford University, the chairman of the national academy's committee.

"Although such experiments are likely to facilitate the solution of important theoretical and practical biological problems, they would also result in the creation of novel types of infectious DNA elements whose biological properties cannot be completely predicted in advance," the committee reports in a Science magazine issue to be published Friday.

"Many expert investigators have ex-

See DNA   Col. 4

The Washington Post, July 18, 1974

AN INDEPENDENT NEWSPAPER

The Scientific Conscience

EVER SINCE HIROSHIMA, scientists have been concerned that probing the secrets of nature with-out caution and moral restraint might open a Pandora box of ills, if not disasters, that could do terrible dam-age. But who is to be the keeper of the keys? Who could be presumed to possess the wisdom to decide what secrets might be unlocked and what had better not be tampered with? Nature knows neither good nor evil. The same discovery or intervention that might do harm might also bring new blessings. Scientific research and experimentation is surely not a matter for the police to control. The best we can hope for is that the collective conscience of scientists themselves asserts itself to weigh the risks in each specific instance.

New York Times

POSSIBLE DANGER HALTS GENE TESTS

Copyright The Washington Post

NEW YORK, THURSDAY, JULY 18, 1974

Genetic Tests Renounced Over Possible Hazards

© 1974 by The New York Times Company. Reprinted by permission.

(Continued from previous pages.)

As scientists, we shall have to spend more time educating the public, not only about our idealistic dreams, say to conquer the common cold or cancer, but also with regard to the old-fashioned idea
on which I was brought up, that the pursuit of knowledge about
the nature of life and about the universe in which it exists is a glo-
rious endeavor that should be undertaken for its own sake.[22]

The Laboratory's *Annual Report* had been published since 1924. On becoming Director in 1968, Watson expanded the section written by the Director beyond the customary highlights of the Laboratory's year, using it as an opportunity to address scientific themes of social and political import. He wrote these essays to articulate molecular biology and its implications for human health to the general public, to argue for his point of view, to discuss strategies for scientific advance in both the scientific and political arenas, and to challenge his audience to think about the ethical and social issues raised by new advances in biology while retaining a cautious optimism about science and scientists. The themes of these essays, written between 1968 and 1998, were diverse, and included fraud in scientific research, the rise of the scientist–business entrepreneur, viruses and cancer, the influence of industry funds in research, and genes and politics.

1968 *Annual Report.* In 1968, Watson became Director of the Cold Spring Harbor Laboratory of Quantitative Biology. In his first Director's Report he expressed a debt of gratitude to John Cairns, who in five years as Director "once again made the Laboratory a going concern." Watson then set out his plans for the future of the Lab, which "is and must be the place where trends of the future are anticipated." The publication ran to 31 pages in 1968 and listed a staff of 35, as well as 12 members of the Genetics Research Unit of the Carnegie Institution of Washington, among them Barbara McClintock.

COLD SPRING HARBOR LABORATORY

ANNUAL
REPORT
1973

1973 *Annual Report.* The cover, in black and white, shows Cold Spring Harbor after an ice storm. The report was 88 pages long and listed a Laboratory staff of more than 100 research scientists, post-doctoral fellows, graduate students, and others, including a "Publications Department" of three.

Watson's forthrightness, his humor and sarcasm, and his use of metaphor characterize these essays, perhaps more so than in his other writings. These elements of his style are, if anything, heightened by the confidence and authority with which he writes. As Walter Gratzer notes in the introduction to a recently published collection of Watson's essays entitled *A Passion for DNA: Genes, Genomes, and Society,*

> *[w]hether or not you agree with his reasons and embrace his conclusions, you will find in his writings the most lucid and authoritative statements for the defense [against the arguments of those] who see moral dilemmas and physical threats all around them . . .*[23]

As a founding father of DNA, Watson had participated in the recombinant DNA controversy, and this topic was the principal focus of his Director's Reports from 1976 and 1979. Two topics, however, emerged as Watson's most frequent themes: the war on cancer and the Human Genome Project. Both were scientific enterprises requiring large sums of public money, but Watson's attitude toward them was very different.

". . . we must realize that high-quality cancer research is likely to be more difficult to pull off than most other forms of biology."
JDW, *PASSION FOR DNA*, P. 136

When President Richard Nixon signed the National Cancer Act in 1971 and announced the "war on cancer," he hoped to raise an American spirit cast down by assassinations, Vietnam, and Watergate. Congress massively increased federal funding for cancer research. But a handful of scientific leaders cautioned against promising the American public a victory that most knew could probably not be soon delivered. Watson was one. From the outset his commentary was provocative:

> *So we must wonder to what extent the current American hysteria to conquer cancer within the next decade arises from the feeling that an infirmity which strikes without respect for social, racial, or economic class must be an easier objective than a moral cancer which grows out of a nation's incapacity to acknowledge the conveniently remote victims of its surgical bombing strikes.*[24]

This scrutiny did not spare the scientists. Was their enthusiasm motivated by a genuine interest in solving the problem of cancer? Watson was troubled by the creation of big science by big money, cautioning that research dominated by large groups might threaten individual creativity. He also asked if the time was ripe for a massive assault on a biological problem as complex—and possibly as intractable—as cancer. In the 1973 Director's Report he wrote:

> *To the biochemist cancer now stands out like Mount Everest did to the alpinists of the late 1940s. Most certainly not the first very tall mountain to surmount, but something you always know is there and if you are strong and calm and make all the right advance prepara-*

DIRECTOR'S REPORT

To the biochemist cancer now stands out like Mount Everest did to the alpinists of the late 1940's. Most certainly not the first very tall mountain to surmount, but something you always know is there and if you are strong and calm and make all the right advance preparations and then are more than a little lucky, you might with the help of many trained companions get to the top. You know all too well that you should wait for the right moment and not set off prematurely without knowing well the terrain of the lower crevasses. Too many of your friends, fresh from the successes of late youth, have started out without maps only to vanish from real science, leaving merely the remains of faded house organs containing smiling faces that have never grasped the essence of the enemy.

We wonder, of course, whether we will land in the same icy graveyard. Those who have disappeared before were not always silly and short-sighted but often scientists of the first rank, with no tolerance for the shoddy optimism of the second-rate. When last seen, however, they usually had become preoccupied with minor facts that had the smell of the irrelevant but which somehow had become that instant's great white hope in the fight against cancer. So today many respectable scientists still consider cancer research synonymous with lousy science. Whenever a well-known scientist announces that he has become interested in cancer, the stock reflex is to regard him as another cop-out, no longer good enough to compete for the increasingly limited money that goes for pure science, and so of necessity he is forced into the bountiful jaws of an overfunded National Cancer Institute.

Our problem, of course, is not whether uninformed outsiders regard us as has-beens, but whether our great effort of the past five years in reorganizing much of this Lab toward tumor virus research will pay off. Could we have jumped in too early, with a massive push toward the molecular nature of cancer only making sense when some totally unanticipated discovery at last gives cancer research an intellectual basis? Or if there already exist some real ideas to test, were there already enough good laboratories committed to their exploration? Did we enter an already overpopulated area of research or was there a vacuum waiting to be filled with intelligent minds?

My prejudiced guess is that in 1969 we chose the right time to go all out. The development in the early 1960's of cell culture techniques for the study of tumor viruses had at long last made technically feasible the study of cancer at the molecular level. The situation was in many ways similar to that of the phage world of 1945, then open for outside invasion because of the pioneering efforts of Delbruck, Hershey and Luria. Thanks to much patient work in a small number of far-sighted research groups (those of Dulbecco Eagle, Green, Rubin, Stoker and Puck quickly come to mind) cancer research was becoming a proper target for the molecular biologist. Yet for a variety of reasons, many connected to the widespread fatalism about the future American commitment to science engendered by the Vietnamese war, almost no new research groups were rising to the challenge. So we did not see how we could fail to leave our mark, that is, if we could get going on a large enough scale.

Key to our initial optimism were hints, now solidly confirmed, that an essential aspect of viral carcinogenesis was the insertion of one or more of the genes of the various tumor viruses into the chromosome(s) of the respective host cells. Here they must code for one or more specific proteins whose presence upsets the normal cellular metabolism, somehow changing it into a cancer cell. Given this way of thinking, the obvious question becomes how to find out the exact biochemical function(s) carried out by these cancer genes. Is always the same task involved or do different cancer viruses bring about cancer in fundamentally different ways? Answering this question, however, is not at all straightforward, and at pessimistic moments can seem like looking for a needle in a haystack. Most of the time, however, we think we have a fighting chance for we focus on the fact that the chromosomes of most known tumor viruses are

4

Watson's 1973 Director's Report discussed cancer research and encouraged the use of government cancer money, particularly in setting up research laboratories in academic universities. The report concluded: "The thought that cooperation between large groups may not only be helpful but also necessary if we are to understand cancer appears to require still another retreat from the Thoreau-like freedom we like to dream about. But we should remember that until they were almost to the summit, Hillary and Tensing were part of a large, well-organized group effort. And the mountain we aim to conquer is probably much higher."

tions and then are more than a little lucky, you might with the help
of many trained companions get to the top. You know all too well that
you should wait for the right moment and not set out prematurely
without knowing well the terrain of the lower crevasses.[25]

His view presaged the more widespread sober realization later in the 1970s that this war would be protracted and very expensive. Eventually, however, Watson came to recognize that the war on cancer was symbolic of a newly emerging era in biological research. Though remaining critical in his assessments, he endorsed increased financial resources for accelerating research, asserting that knowledge gained from the study of simple bacterial and bacteriophage model systems was now ripe for application to more complex organisms, including humans.

In his 1980 Director's Report, Watson's assessment of the war on cancer was more subdued:

As with most battles that go on too long, the hoopla and bravado
are now muted, and the charismatic generals who were to lead us
to certain victory have been rotated to less conspicuous channels.[26]

"Initially, prospecting for DNA was a civilized affair. . . . " JDW, DIRECTOR'S REPORT, 1987

In his essays Watson reflected extensively on how the science of molecular biology had changed from a leisurely intellectual pursuit practiced by a small number of pioneers more or less in constant touch with one another during 1953–1963 to the gigantic industry of the late 1980s. He used the metaphor of DNA as "gold" (recalling that Francis Crick "called his newly expanded row house in Cambridge 'The Golden Helix'")[27] and likened the charge to mine DNA for profit to the California gold rush of the late 1840s. In 1987 he wrote:

Initially, prospecting for DNA was a civilized affair, and the pace
of our daily lives did not measurably change through the remainder
of the 1950s and even into the mid-1960s. Important discoveries
occurred frequently enough to keep our minds alert, but not so often
that long summer vacations in the mountains or on the beaches

1984 *Annual Report.* The cover, in four-color, shows a view of the Laboratory from the Harbor. The report was now 340 pages long and listed a Laboratory staff of more than 300.

would fall victim to fears that new discoveries would blow our labs out of the water. . . . [But now t]he DNA world . . . is no longer a collection of friends who have grown up with each other and know each other's strengths and weaknesses. Instead, none of us can personally know more than a small fraction of our peers.[28]

Watson also castigated the growing ranks of "biotech" entrepreneurs and consultants whose minds were often more on their bank balances than on their experiments.

". . . the ability to look at their [genes'] precise individual forms will provide ever more important tools for predicting the future course of given human lives." JDW, *PASSION FOR DNA*, P. 169

Another important topic for Watson was the Human Genome Project, and he commented often on the efforts and implications of sequenc-

Handwritten manuscript of the 1987 Director's Report. (Courtesy of the James D. Watson Collection, Cold Spring Harbor Laboratory Archives.) The report begins: "The recombinant DNA age is now 15 years old. During this brief period the doing of biological research has changed beyond recognition, and the ability to manipulate DNA has industrial and agricultural consequences that modern nations can ignore only at the expense of their long-term futures. Even more important, DNA research is beginning to have medical and ethical consequences that will affect how we lead our daily lives and plan for the future of our children and they for their children's future."

The Eugenics Record Office of the Carnegie Institute. Built in 1914 to house staff and records, it replaced the Stewart House, where the Office was originally set up in 1910. The brick building in Laurel Hollow became a private residence when it was finally closed in 1940, soon after its director, Henry Laughlin, was persuaded to retire. By then the Carnegie Institute was no longer supporting the work. (Courtesy of Cold Spring Harbor Laboratory Archives.)

ing the entire three billion base pairs in the human genome. So when he became Associate Director of the Office of Human Genome Research in 1988 (he became Director of the National Center for Human Genome Research in 1989, a position he held until 1992), he had already thought and written extensively about the project and was in a unique position both to guide the scientific effort and to examine its ethical aspects. And in his 1985 Director's Report he foreshadowed what would soon become one of the largest government-funded scientific endeavors:

> . . . *we must begin to consider the consequences of our newly found abilities to analyze human DNA molecules, capabilities that over the next several decades should witness the working out of the complete sequence of the some 3×10^9 base pairs that comprise the human genome.*[29]

His report in the following year acknowledged that the project would conceivably consume several billion dollars and some 30,000 scientist-years and that its potential for running out of control and diverting money from other research worried many scientists. To Watson, however, it was irresponsible not to grasp for the goal of a human DNA sequence that would help locate the genes for intractable diseases like cystic fibrosis, muscular dystrophy, and schizophrenia.[30]

". . . there now exists justifiable concern that we may be opening a Pandora's box." JDW, PASSION FOR DNA, P. 169

Watson saw the Human Genome Project as an opportunity for extensive international cooperation and was optimistic that its success would open a new era of intellectual excitement as the messages of the genome were read.[31] In 2000, he was an honored participant in the international celebration of the Project's successful completion.

His responsibility for heading the Human Genome Project prompted Watson to reflect on the ethical implications of this new direction in DNA research. In 1996, his contribution to the Laboratory's *Annual Report* was about the social consequences of genetics,

Walter Gratzer, long-time friend of Watson, who wrote the Introduction and Afterword to Watson's collection of essays, *A Passion for DNA.* He concludes in the Afterword: "The *enfant terrible* at 70 has lost none of his evangelical enthusiasm for science and its uses; he is still captivated by the beautiful molecule DNA that his work with Crick erected as an icon for our age, and by the richness and promise of the science that has flowed from their discovery." (Photograph courtesy of Walter Gratzer.)

including the eugenics movement that had had a significant presence at the Laboratory itself where Charles Davenport, Director of the Carnegie Institute of Washington at Cold Spring Harbor, had established a Eugenics Record Office in 1910. In this essay, Watson recounts the genocidal horrors of Nazi Germany, emphasizing that recognition of the full extent of these horrors generated "disgust for the pseudoscientific theories of race superiority and purity that underpinned Nazi ideology," and noting that "[a]nyone subsequently calling himself a eugenicist put his reputation as a decent moral human at risk.[32]

Two years later, Cold Spring Harbor Laboratory Press reprinted the English translation of Benno Müller-Hill's 1984 book, *Murderous Science: Elimination by Scientific Selection of Jews, Gypsies, and Others in Germany, 1933–1945*.[33] Watson contributed an Afterword to the reprint entitled "Five Days in Berlin"[34] giving an account of his visit to Germany to address the Congress of Molecular Medicine. A representative of the German Ministry of Science preceding him at the podium extolled the lucrative financial potential for Germany in recombinant DNA research and biotechnology. Incensed, Watson quickly modified his prepared remarks:

> *This was not the occasion for her to portray genes as potential servants of the commercial interests of the German state. Instead, she should be*

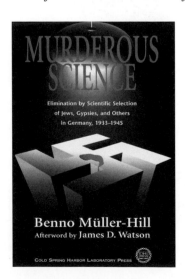

Murderous Science: Elimination by Scientific Selection of Jews, Gypsies, and Others in Germany, 1933–1945 was reprinted in 1998 by Cold Spring Harbor Laboratory Press. The original book was published in Germany in 1984 by a former postdoctoral fellow in Watson's lab, Benno Müller-Hill. An English translation had been published in 1988 by Oxford University Press, but was out of print. Watson was eager to see the book brought back into print and contributed an Afterword to the reprint entitled "Five Days in Berlin."

*emphasizing . . . the desire of the people of the world to find new ways
to combat the pernicious effects of gene-related diseases.*[35]

Watson confronted his audience with the sordid history of the eugenics movement and deplored the postwar whitewash of misdeeds by German geneticists during the Nazi era. He challenged "the German genetics community to finally admit that they [were] deeply ashamed of their forebearers' past"[36] and thus enter the genome era.

"Many of these essays remain highly relevant today . . ." JDW, PREFACE, *PASSION FOR DNA*

In 1999, after Watson decided to stop writing contributions to the Lab's Annual Report, John Inglis, the Director of Cold Spring Harbor Laboratory Press, proposed to Watson a book that would be an anthology of his essays. Walter Gratzer, Emeritus Professor of Biophysical

Errol Friedberg (*left*) and John Inglis (*right*) examining the handwritten Foreword to this book by Sydney Brenner. Dr. Inglis, Executive Director of Cold Spring Harbor Laboratory Press since 1987, has expanded the publishing program to include, in addition to laboratory manuals and scientific monographs, five research journals, textbooks, and children's and general interest titles. In 2003, the Press had almost 50 staff members.

Chemistry at London University and long a friend of Watson, was invited to write a Foreword that set the scene for the essays. After doing so, he got back a note saying, "That's fine. Now please write a post-script indicating the state of molecular biology in cancer research."[37] What emerged was an Afterword entitled "Envoi—DNA, Peace and Laughter."[38]

Cold Spring Harbor Laboratory Press published the essay collection entitled *A Passion for DNA: Genes, Genomes, and Society* (dedicated to Watson's sons Rufus and Duncan) in 2000. Oxford University Press published the U.K. edition.[39] Six of the essays, initially delivered as lectures, were published for the first time. The U.S. paperback edition of *A Passion for DNA* published in 2001 included three new essays: one the text of Watson's Liberty Medal Address in Philadelphia on July 4, 2000, the second the Foreword to a reprint of *Nature's* human genome issue in book form, and a third called "Rules for Graduates."

A Passion for DNA: Genes, Genomes, and Society, published in 2000 by Cold Spring Harbor Laboratory Press, assembled a selection of Watson's best essays on recombinant DNA, the war on cancer, and the societal implications of the Human Genome Project. It also included a section of personal essays, "Autobiographical Flights." The cover photo of Watson was taken by Bill Geddes. Three additional essays were added to the paperback edition, published in 2001.

This collection of Watson's essays was well received. The *Journal of the American Medical Association* called them "stunning,"[40] and *The New England Journal of Medicine* referred to Watson as "the prose laureate'" of biomedical sciences.[41] The *Nature Genetics* reviewer noted that the collection was "generously strewn with the . . . opinionated pronouncements . . . expect[ed] from 'Honest Jim.'"[42] David Weatherall noted in *Science* that the essays demonstrated how untroubled Watson was by his exceptional early achievements.[43] In a similar vein, Sydney Brenner observed in *Nature* that

> *Jim never rested on his laurels, nor did he ever relax his vigilance, finding the enemies of science and dealing with their pomposity and inanity. He also assumed the unlikely role of statesman, and the international human genome sequencing programme owes its existence to Jim's skill in converting most of its early opponents and to his shrewd understanding of Washington politicians. He has used his considerable reputation in the service of science and it is this that has given him the right to make many of the outrageous statements (all carefully calculated) about the war on cancer, the dangers of recombinant DNA, cloning people and other follies of modern science.[44]*

Notes

1. D. Soll and M. Singer, letter to U.S. National Academy of Sciences, July 17, 1973. 1981. In *The DNA story: A documentary history of gene cloning* (ed. J.D. Watson and J. Tooze), pp. 5–6. W.H. Freeman, San Francisco.
2. J.D. Watson. 1977. Director's Report. In *Cold Spring Harbor Laboratory Annual Report*, p. 5. Cold Spring Harbor Laboratory, Cold Spring Harbor, New York.
3. J.D. Watson. 1977. Director's Report. In *Cold Spring Harbor Laboratory Annual Report*, p. 6. Cold Spring Harbor Laboratory, Cold Spring Harbor, New York.
4. J.D. Watson. 1978. Director's Report. In *Cold Spring Harbor Laboratory Annual Report*, p. 6. Cold Spring Harbor Laboratory, Cold Spring Harbor, New York.
5. J.D. Watson and J. Tooze. 1981. In *The DNA story: A documentary history of gene cloning*, p. x. W.H. Freeman, San Francisco.
6. Interview with James D. Watson, March 12, 2003.
7. Interview with Neil Patterson, March 17, 2003.
8. Interview with John Tooze, March 10, 2003.
9. J.D. Watson and J. Tooze. 1981. Prologue. In *The DNA story: A documentary history of gene cloning*, p. x. W.H. Freeman, San Francisco.

10. J.D. Watson and J. Tooze. 1981. Prologue. In *The DNA story: A documentary history of gene cloning*, p. xii. W.H. Freeman, San Francisco.

11. J.D. Watson and J.Tooze. 1981. Epilogue. In *The DNA story: A documentary history of gene cloning*, p. 584. W.H. Freeman, San Francisco.

12. C. Grobstein. 1981. *The San Diego Union*, October 18.

13. H.J. Geiger. 1981. *Science '81*. **2(9):** 124–125.

14. R. Goodell. 1982. Two views about the safety of genetic engineering. *Philadelphia Inquirer*, February 7.

15. G.S. Stent. 1982. The DNA Story: A Documented History of Gene Cloning: Tall stories about DNA. *Cell* **28:** 423–425.

16. J.D. Watson. 1973. When worlds collide: Research and know-nothingism. *The New York Times Op-Ed*, March 22.

17. J.D. Watson. 1977. In defense of DNA. The *New Republic*, June 25, **170:** 11–14; J.D. Watson. 1979. DNA folly continues. *The New Republic*, January 13, **180:** 12.

18. J.D. Watson. 1977. Remarks on recombinant DNA. *CoEvolution Q*, summer, **14:** 40.

19. J.D. Watson. 1979. The DNA biohazard canard. *Time Magazine*, January 31.

20. J.D. Watson. 1978. The Nobelist vs. the film star. *The Washington Post Outlook*, May 14, D1–D2.

21. J.D. Watson. 1979. Let us stop regulating DNA research. *Nature* **278:** 113.

22. J.D. Watson. 1976. Director's Report. In *Cold Spring Harbor Laboratory Annual Report*, p. 14. Cold Spring Harbor Laboratory, Cold Spring Harbor, New York.

23. W. Gratzer. 2000. Introduction. In *A passion for DNA: Genes, genomes, and society*, p. xx. Cold Spring Harbor Laboratory Press, Cold Spring Harbor, New York.

24. J.D. Watson. 1971. Director's Report. In *Cold Spring Harbor Laboratory Annual Report*, p. 2. Cold Spring Harbor Laboratory, Cold Spring Harbor, New York.

25. J.D. Watson. 1973. Director's Report. Director's Report. In *Cold Spring Harbor Laboratory Annual Report*, p. 4. Cold Spring Harbor Laboratory, Cold Spring Harbor, New York.

26. J.D. Watson. 1987. Director's Report. In *Cold Spring Harbor Laboratory Annual Report*, p. 6. Cold Spring Harbor Laboratory, Cold Spring Harbor, New York.

27. J.D. Watson. 1987. Director's Report. In *Cold Spring Harbor Laboratory Annual Report*, p. 8. Cold Spring Harbor Laboratory, Cold Spring Harbor, New York.

28. J.D. Watson. 1987. Director's Report. In *Cold Spring Harbor Laboratory Annual Report*, p. 1. Cold Spring Harbor Laboratory, Cold Spring Harbor, New York.

29. J.D. Watson. 1985. Director's Report. In *Cold Spring Harbor Laboratory Annual Report*, p. 1. Cold Spring Harbor Laboratory, Cold Spring Harbor, New York.

30. J.D. Watson. 1986. Director's Report. In *Cold Spring Harbor Laboratory Annual Report*, p. 1. Cold Spring Harbor Laboratory, Cold Spring Harbor, New York.

31. J.D. Watson. 1986. Director's Report. In *Cold Spring Harbor Laboratory Annual Report*, p. 5. Cold Spring Harbor Laboratory, Cold Spring Harbor, New York.

32. J.D. Watson. 1996. Genes and Politics. President's Essay. In *Cold Spring Harbor Laboratory Annual Report*, p. 10. Cold Spring Harbor Laboratory, Cold Spring Harbor, New York.

33. B. Müller-Hill. 1988. *Murderous science: Elimination by scientific selection of Jews, Gypsies, and others in Germany, 1933–1945*. Oxford University Press, London.

34. J.D. Watson. 1998. Five days in Berlin. In *Murderous science: Elimination by scientific selection of Jews, Gypsies, and others in Germany, 1933–1945* (by B. Müller-Hill), pp. 187–200. Cold Spring Harbor Laboratory Press, Cold Spring Harbor, New York.

35. J.D. Watson. 1998. Five days in Berlin. In *Murderous science: Elimination by scientific selection of Jews, Gypsies, and others in Germany, 1933–1945* (by B. Müller-Hill), p.194. Cold Spring Harbor Laboratory Press, Cold Spring Harbor, New York.

36. J.D. Watson. 1998. Five days in Berlin. In *Murderous science: Elimination by scientific selection of Jews, Gypsies, and others in Germany, 1933–1945* (by B. Müller-Hill), p. 195. Cold Spring Harbor Laboratory Press, Cold Spring Harbor, New York.

37. Interview with Walter Gratzer, March 1, 2003.

38. W. Gratzer. 2000. Envoi—DNA, peace and laughter. In *A passion for DNA: Genes, genomes, and society* (by J.D. Watson), p. 231. Cold Spring Harbor Laboratory Press, Cold Spring Harbor, New York.

39. Watson has not kept any royalties from *A Passion for DNA*. All such payments to him have been gifted back to Cold Spring Harbor Laboratory. Royalties from the Oxford University Press editions have been gifted back to Clare College.

40. D.W. Hodo. 2001. *J. Am. Med. Assoc.* **285:** 342.

41. D.A. Chambers. 2000. *N. Engl. J. Med.* **343:** 370.

42. K. Davies. 2000. The helix files. *Nat. Genet.* **25:** 23.

43. D. Weatherall. 2000. Was there life after DNA? *Science* **289:** 554–555.

44. S. Brenner. 2000. The house that Jim built. *Nature* **405:** 511–512.

DNA: The Secret
of Life

"My mother . . . believed in genes. She was proud of her father's Scottish origins, and saw in him the traditional Scottish virtues of honesty, hard work, and thriftiness. She, too, possessed these qualities and felt that they must have been passed down to her from him." JDW, *DNA: The Secret of Life*, Chap. 1, p. 3

During the 1980s, Publisher Neil Patterson raised with Watson the possibility of producing a set of videos and animations on DNA.[1] Watson was not interested at the time. But in the late 1990s, aware that the 50th anniversary of the discovery of the structure of DNA was imminent, Watson suggested a book on DNA with accompanying video that would convey to the widest audience possible the excitement and social importance of DNA science. A project was set in motion that included a serialized TV documentary on DNA, a book to complement the TV production, and other educational projects. It was an opportunity to educate the general public about scientific and medical advances in genetics, and their social and political implications—an opportunity that with his interest in education and advocacy Watson was bound to seize—and, with his record of achievement, who better to seize it?

The 50th Anniversary of the discovery of the structure of DNA was celebrated in a special issue of *Nature*, January 23, 2003 (Vol. 421, No. 6921). It contained facsimile papers from the *Nature* April 25, 1953 issue, as well as a section of historical perspectives, and articles on DNA in medicine and society and on DNA, the biological molecule. (Reprinted with permission from *Nature*.)

Asilomar revisited: filming for the TV series in 2003. Watson (*second from right*) and film crew in front of the conference building that hosted the first Asilomar conference in 1973 and the more famous Asilomar conference in 1975, where scientists opened up concerns about the possible dangers of recombinant DNA research for public scrutiny and comment. (Photo courtesy of Jan Witkowski.)

Watson (*left*) with Andrew Berry (*standing*). As an author team, the two worked together well. Berry was originally enlisted to work on the TV series, "DNA," but proved an ideal coauthor for the book. (Photo courtesy of Jan Witkowski.)

". . . it is JDW's personal view and is accordingly written in the first person singular." AUTHORS' NOTE, *DNA: THE SECRET OF LIFE*, P. IX

Andrew Berry of Harvard's Museum of Comparative Zoology, a seasoned biologist and an accomplished writer, had been hired to write the TV script. But Berry was also an appropriate coauthor of the book to accompany the series. The book, as far as Watson was concerned, was the real medium for his message.[2]

Working together, Berry and Watson had extensive conversations about what Watson wanted to see in a particular chapter, Berry wrote the chapter, and then Watson reviewed it, either simply correcting the occasional word or providing extensive critiques of the form, balance, and content, particularly in the more personal sections.[3] Watson rewrote much of the chapter on the discovery of the double helix and he wrote the Coda: Our Genes and Our Future entirely himself.[4]

By the spring of 2002, Berry had completed drafts of four or five chapters. By the summer, Watson's focus on the book had sharpened and the pace accelerated through meetings and phone calls. The difficulties of dual authorship were diminished both by Watson's grace in dealing with a junior author and by Berry's willingness to serve as a mouthpiece for Watson's opinions.[5] Stylistic differences were resolved by the book's editor George Andreou of A.A. Knopf, whom Watson and Berry acknowledged "wrote much more of this book—the good bits—than either of us would ever let on."[6] Andreou's expertise was

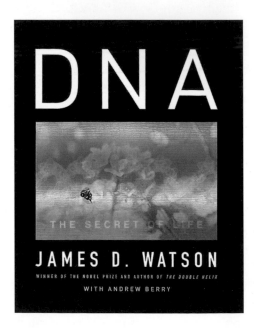

DNA: The Secret of Life was published by A.A. Knopf in April 2003. The cover features a hologram showing flowers and a bee in one view (by Mika Minagawa) and an image of a double helix in another. In the Authors' Note, Watson and coauthor Berry write: "Taking the fiftieth anniversary as an opportunity to pause and take stock of where we are, we give an unabashedly personal view both of the history and of the issues." (From *DNA*, by James D. Watson, ©2003 by DNA Show LLC. Used by permission of Alfred A. Knopf, a division of Random House.)

underscored by a reviewer who commented, "Anyone who has ever heard [Watson] speak, in conversation or lecture, will feel his presence throughout."[7]

". . . someone with zero biological knowledge should be able to understand the book's every word." AUTHORS' NOTE, *DNA: THE SECRET OF LIFE*, P. X

DNA: The Secret of Life was published by A.A. Knopf in April 2003, 50 years to the month since Watson and Crick's paper suggesting a structure for DNA. The year 2003 was filled with events, exhibits, meetings, interviews, and books celebrating the discovery of the double helix and examining the progress in molecular biology since 1953.

DNA: The Secret of Life is dedicated to Francis Crick (the only individual acknowledged twice in this manner by Watson). The book owes its name to "[Francis] Crick's brag in the Eagle, the pub [in Cambridge, England] where we habitually ate lunch, that we had indeed discovered 'the secret of life.'"[8] The title also resonates with that of the very influential book written in the 1940s by the physicist Erwin Schrödinger entitled *What is Life?*, the work that was eagerly read by Watson, Crick, and many others. (This book's cover is shown at the beginning of Chapter 2, entitled, "The Double Helix: This Is Life.") It is this book that got Watson "hooked on the gene."[9]

The intention was that "someone with zero biological knowledge should be able to understand the book's every word."[10] Thus the book is characterized by a design that gives the general reader the bare minimum of basic biology to comprehend the links between the science of DNA and genetics and its impact on society. *DNA: The Secret of Life* touches on just about every aspect of DNA biology, with chapters on the history of genetics (including eugenics), the discovery of the double helix in 1953, gene cloning, genetic engineering of foods, the Human Genome Project, evolution, DNA fingerprinting, and genetic

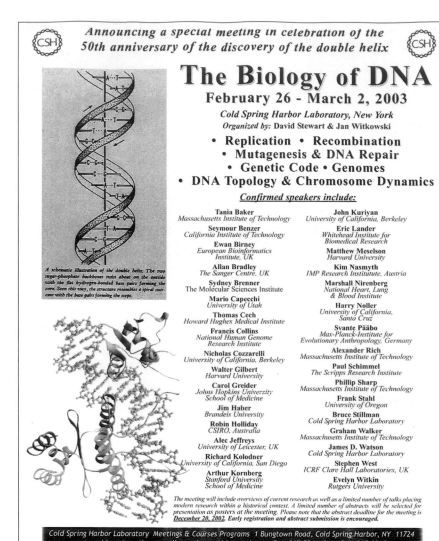

Fiftieth Anniversary Events. (*This page*) "The Biology of DNA" was a special conference held at Cold Spring Harbor Laboratory, February 26–March 3, 2003, and organized by David Stewart and Jan Witkowski. (Courtesy of Cold Spring Harbor Laboratory Meetings & Courses.) (*Facing page, top*) Conference participants. The conference was held as part of a larger "DNA Week" in New York City that included exhibits and lectures and other public events. (*Bottom*) The exhibit "'Honest Jim': James Watson, the Writer" was assembled from the James D. Watson Collection of the Cold Spring Harbor Laboratory Archive and organized by Mila Pollock. It was shown at the New York Public Library of Science, Technology, and Business for three months. (Courtesy of Cold Spring Harbor Laboratory Library.)

Left to right: Norton Zinder, Watson, Bruce Stillman, Phil Sharp, Rodney Rothstein, Waclaw Szybalski, and Ham Smith at The Biology of DNA Conference. Liz Watson is on left in second row. (Courtesy of the Cold Spring Harbor Laboratory Archives.)

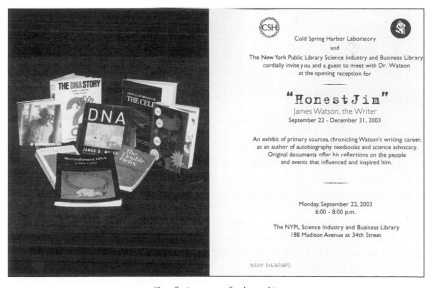

(See facing page for legend.)

Gala Celebration. (*Top*) The Waldorf-Astoria Gala, held on February 28, 2003, 50 years to the day the discovery was made, was a by-invitation-only black tie affair, attended by scientists and celebrities and hosted by Charlie Rose. (*Harbor Transcript*, Spring/Fall 2003. Cold Spring Harbor Laboratory.) (*Bottom*) Scientists attending Cold Spring Harbor meetings always dress very casually and were amused at having to wear tuxedos for the Gala dinner. *Left to right:* Robin Holliday, Errol Friedberg (the author), Miroslav Radman, Sir Alec Jeffreys, and James Haber. (Photo courtesy of Errol Friedberg.)

CONTENTS

· · ·

vii

The Table of Contents of *DNA: The Secret of Life* shows the range of topics covered, from the beginning of genetics in Mendel's studies of peas through the discovery of the double helix and the working out of the human genome. The first 50 years of the DNA revolution brought remarkable scientific progress as well as the initial application of that progress to human problems. Watson and Berry wrote the book for a general audience with "zero knowledge" of biology. (From *DNA*, by James D. Watson, ©2003 by DNA Show LLC. Used by permission of Alfred A. Knopf, a division of Random House.)

diseases, as well as the numerous sociological, ethical, financial, legal, medical, and evolutionary implications of DNA. It is rich in photographs, diagrams, and figures.

Watson advances his opinions throughout, asking—and answering—questions previously addressed to the more limited readership of his essays and *The DNA Story*. What are the dangers of genetic engineering? Should professors be permitted to enrich themselves on the basis of work done in their university's facilities? Would the commercialization of academic science create irreconcilable conflicts of interest?[11] The impact of DNA on our understanding of human biology is also discussed.

Because humans are 99.9% identical genetically, what does it mean that human variations do not correlate with "race" defined by skin color and other physical characteristics? In a chapter on genetic fin-

The Double Helix

It was quite a moment. We felt sure that this was it. Anything that simple, that elegant just had to be right. What got us most excited was the complementarity of the base sequences along the two chains. If you knew the sequence—the order of bases—along one chain, you automatically knew the sequence along the other. It was immediately apparent that this must be how the genetic messages of genes are copied so exactly when chromosomes duplicate prior to cell division. The molecule would "unzip" to form two separate strands. Each separate strand then could serve as the template for the synthesis of a new strand, one double helix becoming two.

In *What Is Life?* Schrödinger had suggested that the language of life might be like Morse code, a series of dots and dashes. He wasn't far off. The language of DNA is a linear series of As, Ts, Gs, and Cs. And just as transcribing a page out

The insight that made it all come together: complementary pairing of the bases

D N A

University lab, Benzer produced a map of a single bacteriophage gene, *rII*, showing how a series of mutations—all errors in the genetic script—were laid out linearly along the virus DNA. The language was simple and linear, just like a line of text on the written page.

The response of the Hungarian physicist Leo Szilard to my Cold Spring Harbor talk on the double helix was less academic. His question was, "Can you patent it?" At one time Szilard's main source of income had been a patent that he held with Einstein, and he had later tried unsuccessfully to patent with Enrico Fermi the nuclear reactor they built at the University of Chicago in 1942. But then as now patents were given only for useful inventions and at the time no one could conceive of a practical use for DNA. Perhaps then, Szilard suggested, we should copyright it.

53

There remained, however, a single missing piece in the double helical jigsaw puzzle: our unzipping idea for DNA replication had yet to be experimentally verified. Max Delbrück, for example, was unconvinced. Though he liked the double helix as a model, he worried that unzipping it might generate horrible knots. Five years later, a former student of Pauling's, Matt Meselson, and the equally bright young phage worker Frank Stahl put to rest such fears when they published the results of a single elegant experiment.

They had met in the summer of 1954 at the Marine Biological Laboratory at Woods Hole, Massachusetts, where I was then lecturing, and agreed—over a good many gin martinis—that they should get together to do some science. The

DNA replication: the double helix is unzipped and each strand copied.

58

Keith Roberts, who had first done illustrations for Watson's *Molecular Biology of the Gene*, published in 1965, produced 18 drawings for *DNA: The Secret of Life*. (*Top*) The illustration on p. 53 is captioned: "The insight that made it all come together: complementary pairing of the bases." (*Bottom*) The illustration on p. 58 shows "DNA replication: the double helix is unzipped and each strand copied." (From *DNA*, by James D. Watson, ©2003 by DNA Show LLC. Used by permission of Alfred A. Knopf, a division of Random House.)

The cultural wonder that is Homo sapiens. Two contrasting notions of chic: Paris 1950s and the highlands of Papua New Guinea. Evolutionary psychology seeks the common denominators underlying all our widely divergent behavior.

a newborn, for instance, strong enough that a baby can use its hands and feet to suspend its full body weight, is presumably a legacy from the time when the ability to cling to a hirsute mother was important for infant survival.

Evolutionary psychology does not, however, limit its scope to such mundane faculties. Is the relatively low representation of women in the mathematical sciences worldwide a universal fact of culture, or might eons of evolution have selected male and female brains for different purposes? Can we understand in strictly Darwinian terms the tendency of older men to marry younger women? With a teenager likely to produce more children than a thirty-five-year-old, might such men be seen as succumbing to the power of evolutionary hardwiring that urges each of them to maximize the number of his offspring? Similarly, do younger women go for wealthy older men because natural selection has operated in the past to favor such a preference: a powerful male with plenty of

383

A page from the chapter entitled "Who We Are: Nature vs. Nurture." The caption reads: "The cultural wonder that is *Homo sapiens*. Two contrasting notions of chic: Paris 1950s and the highlands of Papua New Guinea. Evolutionary biology seeks the common denominators underlying all our widely divergent behavior." (From *DNA*, by James D. Watson, ©2003 by DNA Show LLC. Used by permission of Alfred A. Knopf, a division of Random House.)

gerprinting, Watson argues that everyone should provide a DNA sample because the sacrifice of this particular form of anonymity does not seem an unreasonable price to pay for potentially identifying criminals. But there must be strict and judicious control over access to databases because of the possibility of, for example, wrongful imprisonment of an innocent individual.[12]

Discussing "Who We Are: Nature vs. Nurture," Watson admits the "danger of assuming that genes are responsible for differences we see among individuals or groups." He also concedes that "[w]e can err mightily unless we can be confident that environmental factors have not played the more decisive role."[13] He maintains that

> [t]he current epidemic of political correctness has delivered us to a moment when even the possibility of a genetic basis for difference is a hot potato: there is a fundamentally dishonest resistance to admitting the role of our genes in setting one individual apart from another.[14]

In the Coda, Watson, avowedly not religious, cites as an essential truth St. Paul's view that

> *[l]ove, that impulse that promotes our caring for one another, is what permitted our survival and success on this planet [and] will safeguard our future as we venture into uncharted territory. So fundamental is it to human nature that I am sure that the capacity to love is inscribed in our DNA.*[15]

In this project, Watson took on an unfamiliar writing genre, relied (for the first time) largely on a coauthor, and yet succeeded in producing a book that was original and critically successful. Reviewing the book for *Nature*, Maxine Singer, President Emeritus of the Carnegie Institute of Washington, wrote, "this book is more inclusive and is better reading than similar attempts by science journalists."[16]

Notes

1. Interview with Neil Patterson, March 17, 2003.
2. Interview with Andrew Berry, February 24, 2003.
3. Interview with Andrew Berry, February 24, 2003.
4. Interview with Andrew Berry, February 24, 2003.
5. Interview with Andrew Berry, February 24, 2003.
6. J.D. Watson, with A. Berry. 2003. Authors' Note. In *DNA: The secret of life*, p. x. A.A. Knopf, New York.
7. M. Waldholz. 2003. Ascending the spiral staircase. *Wall Street Journal*, March 28.
8. J.D. Watson, with A. Berry. 2003. Introduction. In *DNA: The secret of life*, p. xii. A.A. Knopf, New York.
9. J.D. Watson, with A. Berry. 2003. In *DNA: The secret of life*, p. 35. A.A. Knopf, New York.
10. J.D. Watson, with A. Berry. 2003. Authors' Note. In *DNA: The secret of life*, p. x. A.A. Knopf, New York.
11. J.D. Watson, with A. Berry. 2003. *DNA: The secret of life*, p. 118, 119. A.A. Knopf, New York.
12. J.D. Watson, with A. Berry. 2003. *DNA: The secret of life*, p. 290. A.A. Knopf, New York.
13. J.D. Watson, with A. Berry. 2003. *DNA: The secret of life*, p. 363. A.A. Knopf, New York.
14. J.D. Watson, with A. Berry. 2003. *DNA: The secret of life*, p. 363. A.A. Knopf, New York.
15. J.D. Watson, with A. Berry. 2003. *DNA: The secret of life*, pp. 404, 405. A.A. Knopf, New York.
16. M. Singer. 2003. Life, the movie. *Nature* **422:** 809–810.

TEXTBOOKS

MOLECULAR BIOLOGY
OF THE GENE

"It is easy to consider man unique among living organisms. He alone has developed complicated languages that allow meaningful and complex interplay of ideas and emotions. . . . Nevertheless, evolutionary theory . . . affects our thinking by suggesting that the basic principles of the living state are the same in all living forms." JDW, MOLECULAR BIOLOGY OF THE GENE, 1E, CHAP. 1

When Watson arrived at Harvard as an Assistant Lecturer in 1956, he found the teaching of biology rooted in the premolecular era. In his opinion, the introductory biology course "abounded in dull facts that were only memorized by its largely premedical attendees. One year its abject dreariness provoked the student-written 'Confidential Guide' to suggest that one of its instructors might best shoot himself."[1]

Despite his recent and junior status on the faculty, Watson was determined to modernize biology at Harvard. He took his teaching duties in introductory biology seriously, investing considerable time and effort in the preparation of his lectures. He gave a set of ten lectures on molecular biology and, discovering there was no text, provided written synopses of his lectures, so that the students could focus on trying to understand his words as he delivered them.[2]

In 1963, Watson accepted an invitation to lecture early in the following year to high school students in Australia, an obligation that

Watson in his Harvard office, 1962. (Courtesy of the Harvard University Archives. Photo credit: Rick Stafford.) Watson was on the Harvard faculty from 1956 to 1976, beginning as Assistant Lecturer in 1956, and then, starting in 1958, as Associate Professor of Biology. He was promoted to Professor of Biology in 1961. He ran a lab in the Harvard BioLabs, working on numerous aspects of how the genetic code was translated to proteins. Later, Wally Gilbert, initially a physicist at Harvard, joined him in his work.

required him to contribute chapters to a multiauthored book eventually called *Light and Life in the Universe*.[3] Watson realized that in his three chapters he had the seeds of an undergraduate textbook, which he initially wanted to call "This Is Life" in response to Erwin Schrödinger's 1944 book "What is Life?"

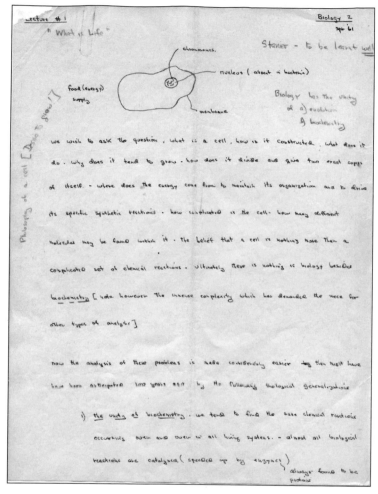

Watson's Course Notes for the Introductory course, Biology 2, Harvard University, 1961. Lecture #1 is entitled "What is Life." The drawing is of a cell. Note to the right says "Biology has the unity of a) evolution b) biochemistry." (Courtesy of the James D. Watson Collection, Cold Spring Harbor Laboratory Archives.)

"I have not only attempted to convey the excitement of the recent discoveries of molecular genetics, but also to relate this new knowledge to the basic problem of biology—the nature of cells and how they divide." JDW, PREFACE, *MOLECULAR BIOLOGY OF THE GENE*, 1E

The recently founded New York publisher, W.A. Benjamin, Inc. (which is today Benjamin Cummings), had offices in a decrepit building at 92nd and Broadway.[4] Benjamin had published a series of physics, chemistry, and biology monographs, and had begun a new series of biology teaching monographs edited by Cyrus Levinthal from the Massachusetts Institute of Technology. In the Editor's Foreword to the series, Levinthal noted that undergraduate biology courses were becoming more and more dependent on physics, mathematics, and chemistry, now more important for a deeper understanding of the subject.[5]

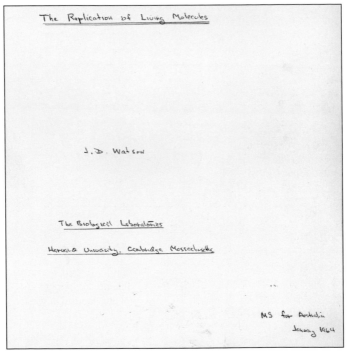

(*This page*) Title page of the manuscript, "The Replication of Living Molecules," written in January 1964 for presentation to high school students in Australia. (*Facing page, top*) Note that, after the introduction, was section 1, entitled "A chemists look at the living cell." The three lectures were subsequently published as three chapters in the little known book, *Light and Life in the Universe.* (*Facing page, bottom*) These chapters formed the basis of the future *[The] Molecular Biology of the Gene*, as the edited title page shows. (Courtesy of the James D. Watson Collection, Cold Spring Harbor Laboratory Archives.)

Introduction

1) A chemists look at the living cell

   a) rapid interconversion of small molecules into useful building blocks

   b) controlled release of energy (degredative vs synthetic reactions)

   c) need for enzymes to catalyse almost all reactions.

   d) construction of very large molecules from sub-units

   e) enormous complexity of proteins + nucleic acids

2) The concept of Template surfaces

   a) chlorophyll synthesis using enzymes to chose correct atoms.

   b) paradox of enzymes to make enzymes - need for self-duplicating template - use of complementary surfaces.

   c) realization that chromosomes control enzyme (protein) structure - store genetic information.

   d) identification of DNA as the genetic (information) component of the chromosome.

   e) establishment of DNA as complementary double helix united by hydrogen bonds.

The Molecular Biology of the Gene

~~The Replication of Living Molecules~~

J. D. Watson

The Biological Laboratories
Harvard University
Cambridge 38, Massachusetts

Copyright 1964

by J. D. Wat——

MS for Australia
January, 1964

(Continued from facing page.)

After a chance meeting at Harvard between Watson and Levinthal, Neil Patterson, Benjamin's young chief editor, lost no time in following up. Watson recalls that

> *[l]ess than a week later [after the chance meeting with Levinthal], its main editor, the young Canadian Neil Patterson, came to my office to make me a Benjamin author like Murray Gell-Mann and Dick Feynman.*[6]

Though impressed by Watson's reputation, Patterson had no knowledge of Watson's writing and had reservations about signing him as an author. Watson realized that Benjamin was far from established, but he liked the way in which Patterson sought out books by clever young scientists.[7] Watson signed a contract for a 125-page monograph on the spot.

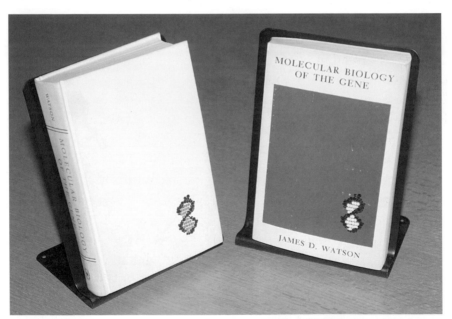

Molecular Biology of the Gene, first edition, was published in 1965 by W.A. Benjamin as part of the Biology Teaching Monograph Series. However, because of its growing length, the trim size was increased from 5 1/2" x 8 1/2" to 6" x 9". In the end the intended 125-page monograph ran to 494 pages in length. (Reproduced with permission from Benjamin Cummings. Photo credit: Phil Renna.)

A crucial and unique element of *Molecular Biology of the Gene* was Watson's inclusion of a historical perspective. The opening chapter, "The Mendelian View of the World," introduced the work of Gregor Mendel and a number of other notable early experimental biologists, including members of T.H. Morgan's "fly room" at Columbia University. But Watson also alluded to more contemporary investigators such as Lawrence Bragg, Linus Pauling, Max Perutz, John Kendrew, Maurice Wilkins, and Rosalind Franklin.

The book also has chapters called "Cells Obey the Laws of Chemistry" and "A Chemist's Look at the Bacterial Cell," another first for a textbook on biology. Having realized the importance of hydrogen bonds in determining the structure of DNA, Watson decided late in the writing of the manuscript that it would be useful to include a chapter on the nature of weak chemical interactions and to show how their weak character makes them indispensable to cellular existence.[8] A final chapter, far ahead of its time, was called "A Geneticist's View of Cancer."

The organization of the book was highly original. Watson introduced the use of sharp and informative headings—he called them "concept heads." The chapter, "The Mendelian View of the World," includes headings that present entire concepts—"Mitosis Maintains the Parental Chromosome Number," "Meiosis Reduces the Parental Chromosome Number," and "Some Genes Are Neither Dominant Nor Recessive." To convey a sense of the extended time it took for X-ray crystallography to yield useful information about the structure of macromolecules, Watson used the heading, "The 25 Year Loneliness of the Protein Crystallographer." And "Avery's Bombshell—Nucleic Acids Can Carry Genetic Specificity" conveys the importance of the experiments by Oswald Avery and his colleagues in the mid-1940s, which showed that genes are made of DNA.

The imaginative and colorful illustrations were an invaluable contribution to the book. Keith Roberts, the illustrator who provided the original drawings, was an English 18-year-old student spending the summer at Harvard before going up to Cambridge University as an

1

THE
MENDELIAN
VIEW OF
THE WORLD

IT IS EASY TO CONSIDER MAN UNIQUE among living organisms. He alone has developed complicated languages that allow meaningful and complex interplay of ideas and emotions. Great civilizations have developed· and changed our world's environment in ways inconceivable for any other form of life. Thus there has always been a tendency to think that something special differentiates man from everything else. This belief has found expression in man's religions, by which he tries to find an origin for his existence and, in so doing, to provide workable rules for conducting his life. It seemed natural to think that, just as every human life begins and ends at a fixed time, man had not always existed but was created at a fixed moment, perhaps the same moment for man and for all other forms of life.

This belief was first seriously questioned just over 100 years ago when Darwin and Wallace proposed their theories of evolution, based upon selection of the most fit. They stated that the various forms of life are not constant, but are continually giving rise to slightly different animals and plants, some of which are adapted to survive and to multiply more effectively. At the time of this theory, they did not know the origin of this continuous variation, but they did correctly realize that these new characteristics must persist in the progeny if such variations were to form the basis of evolution.

1

2   MOLECULAR BIOLOGY OF THE GENE

At first, there was a great deal of furor against Darwin, most of it coming from people who did not like to believe that man and the rather obscene-looking apes could have a common ancestor, even if this ancestor had occurred some 50 to 100 million years in the past. There was also initial opposition from many biologists, who failed to find Darwin's evidence convincing. Among these was the famous Swiss-born naturalist Agassiz, then at Harvard, who spent many years writing against Darwin and Darwin's champion, T. H. Huxley, the most successful of the popularizers of evolution. But by the end of the nineteenth century, the scientific argument was almost finished; both the current geographic distribution of plants and animals and their selective occurrence in the fossil records of the geologic past were explicable only by postulating that continuously evolving groups of organisms had descended from a common ancestor. Today, the theory of evolution is an accepted fact for everyone but a fundamentalist minority, whose objections are based not on reasoning but on doctrinaire adherence to religious principles.

An immediate consequence of the acceptance of Darwinian theory is the realization that life first existed on our Earth some 1 to 2 billion years ago in a simple form, possibly resembling the bacteria—the simplest variety of life now existing. Of course, the very existence of such small bacteria tells us that the essence of the living state is found in very small organisms. Nonetheless, evolutionary theory further affects our thinking by suggesting that the basic principles of the living state are the same in all living forms.

THE CELL THEORY

The same conclusion is independently given by the second great principle of nineteenth century biology, the *cell theory*. This theory, first put forward convincingly in 1839 by the German microscopists Schleiden and Schwann, proposes that all the larger plants and animals are constructed from small fundamental units called cells. All cells are surrounded by a membrane, and usually contain an inner body, the nucleus, which is

(See facing page for legend.)

to form a regular helix and the tendency of the side groups to twist the backbone into a configuration that maximizes the strength of the secondary bonds formed by the side groups.

PROTEIN STRUCTURES ARE USUALLY IRREGULAR

In the case of proteins, the compromise between the side groups and the backbone groups is usually decided in favor of the side groups. Thus, as we shall show in much greater detail in Chapter 6, most amino acids in proteins are not part of regular helices. This is because almost one half of the side groups are nonpolar and can be placed in contact with water only by a considerable input of free energy. This conclusion was at first a surprise to many chemists, who were influenced by the fact that backbone groups could form strong internal hydrogen bonds, whereas the nonpolar groups could form only the much weaker van der Waals bonds. Their past reasoning was faulty, however, because it did not consider either the fact that the polar backbone can form almost as strong external hydrogen bonds to water, or the equally important fact that a significant amount of energy is necessary to push nonpolar side groups into a hydrogen-bonded water lattice.

This argument leads to the interesting prediction that in aqueous solutions macromolecules containing a large number of nonpolar side groups will tend to be more stable than molecules containing mostly polar groups. If we disrupt a polar molecule held together by a large number of internal hydrogen bonds, the decrease in free energy is often small, since the polar groups can then hydrogen bond to water. On the contrary, when we disrupt molecules having many nonpolar groups, there is usually a much greater loss in free energy, because the disruption necessarily inserts nonpolar groups into water.

DNA CAN FORM A REGULAR HELIX

At first glance, DNA looks even more unlikely to form a regular helix than does an irregular polypeptide chain. DNA not only has an irregular sequence of side groups, but in addition, all its side groups are hydrophobic. Both the purines (adenine and

Page 130 shows the interior design of the book as well as the concept heads that helped clarify ideas for the reader: "Protein structures are usually irregular," "DNA can form a regular helix." A revolutionary format at the time, the concept head was used in the organization of all of Watson's subsequent textbooks. (Reproduced with permission from Benjamin Cummings.)

undergraduate. Watson quickly recognized his drawing talent[9] and brought him into the project. Roberts, aware of the prosaic quality of figures in most high school and college texts, developed fundamental rules for his illustrations: no extraneous labels or information in a figure, a single figure had to tell a complete story, and if a figure was too complicated to understand in ten seconds, it was split in two.[10] No one had previously thought of drawing tubes on a simplified centrifuge rotor to convey the notion of centrifugation, or Bunsen burners to connote heating during an experiment. His renderings of cellular substructures such as ribosomes, based on electron micrographs, have become almost universal.[11] The use of a second color (brownish-gold) helped clarify the concepts.

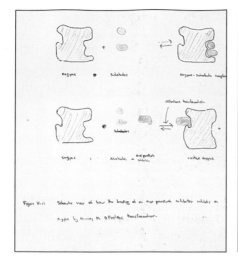

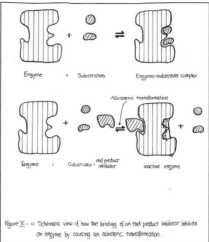

Evolution of an illustration. Two versions by Keith Roberts: (*top left*) a draft of the figure for concept and clarity, and (*top right*) a final drawing for presentation to the artist, showing shading and labels to be typeset. (*Right*) The final, two-color illustration with typeset labels that appeared in the book was prepared by Bill Prokos, Benjamin's illustrator. (Courtesy of the James D. Watson Collection, Cold Spring Harbor Laboratory Archives.) The most important stage was the first, which required both scientific knowledge and understanding of how to present ideas visually. Watson recognized that Keith Roberts had that rare combination of attributes.

Regulation of protein synthesis and function   411

resemble that of the substrate of the inhibited enzyme, so that one would not expect an end-product inhibitor to combine with the enzymatically active site (region that binds the substrate) of the enzyme it inactivates. Instead, there is the suspicion that it reversibly combines in some cases with a second site on the enzyme and yet causes the enzyme activity to be blocked, perhaps by causing a change in the precise enzyme shape (allosteric transformation) and thus preventing the enzyme from combining with its substrate (Figure 14–11). Such proteins, whose shapes are changed by the binding of specific small molecules at sites other than the active site are called *allosteric proteins*, and, correspondingly, those small molecules that bring about allosteric transformations are called *allosteric effectors*. There are now only scant data on the chemical forces binding specific

FIGURE 14–11 *Schematic view of how the binding of an end-product inhibitor inhibits an enzyme by causing an allosteric transformation.*

" . . . I gave it the intellectual flavor that made it a more than meticulous rendering of the new facts of the past decade." JDW, PASSION FOR *DNA*, P. 120

But above all, *Molecular Biology of the Gene* was extraordinary for Watson's engaging writing style—relaxed and pellucid:

> *Since the awakening of an interest in the chemistry of life, a prime challenge has been to understand the generation of energy in a useful form.*[12]

To ensure that the writing was clear enough for the undergraduate, Watson obtained feedback from clever students. One, Dolly Gartner, an English major at Radcliffe, had also taken biology courses, and the litmus test for *Molecular Biology of the Gene* was Dolly Gartner's ability to comprehend the contents of each chapter without seeing the illustrations. "If Dolly was satisfied by words alone, I figured students less bright than she could follow my suitably illustrated arguments."[13]

Watson explained what he was trying to achieve in the Preface:

> *I have not only attempted to convey the excitement of the recent discoveries of molecular genetics, but also to relate this new knowledge to the basic problem of biology—the nature of cells and how they divide. It has, therefore, been necessary to talk about ATP as well as DNA. . . . I am aware, however, that some people may feel that I would have best restricted my discussion to the gene itself, with the expectation that the reader will learn the main principles of intermediary metabolism in another text. . . . When I began to write the first draft, however, I was bothered by the artificial nature of the separation and so decided to start the book with two historically oriented chapters to help the reader see how our ideas about molecular genetics have developed out of the work of the classical geneticists and biochemists.*[14]

What emerged was remarkable—a readable book that synthesized the essential elements of chemistry, biochemistry, and genetics into the new discipline of molecular biology, in a historical context. Neil Patterson described the writing and editorial process:

Jim invented his own editorial arrangement. His manuscript came in promptly and in tidy shape, already read closely, critically, by students he had himself engaged (a first in the business). His diagrams were rendered in draft form by a skillful student, the now famous Keith Roberts (another first—no text author had ever delivered to a publisher such a carefully constructed set of diagrams). It was a publisher's dream. We thought of ourselves as sharp and thorough editors. He left us little to do. He had done it all.[15]

The book's production, however, had its complications. Many of the later chapters required, by Watson's exacting standards, frequent revision, pushing back the original publication date by six months and requiring the first original galleys to be entirely reset at great expense. The publisher threatened to charge Watson for the cost involved, but in the end realized that the changes let them publish an up-to-the-minute textbook.[16] To alert readers to just how current the information in the book was, the publisher included an unusual statement in the front matter of the first edition:

The final chapter of this manuscript was sent to the compositor on 26 January 1965; this volume was published on 21 July 1965.[17]

The first edition of *Molecular Biology of the Gene*, dedicated to Watson's first mentor in science Salvador Luria, was published as a monograph on July 21, 1965.[18] It appeared a year later than the first-ever textbook of molecular biology,[19] but its uniqueness was immediately recognized. Reviewers referred to "the book's outstanding attributes of clarity, with coherence and authenticity."[20]

Rollin Hotchkiss of The Rockefeller University noted that it was "full of insights into such questions as why this or that discovery or viewpoint was difficult to reach or apparently contradicted in earlier times. This is lasting history."[21] The distinguished French molecular biologist François Jacob sent a note to Watson stating, "once I had begun [reading] I couldn't stop until I had finished."[22] His colleague André Lwoff told Benjamin how "a huge and complex set of data has been clearly exposed and organized into an elegant and coherent pic-

W. A. BENJAMIN, INC.
BOOK PUBLISHERS

November 19, 1964

Dr. James D. Watson
Department of Biology
Harvard University
Cambridge 38, Massachusetts

Dear Jim:

The cover sketches and revised chapter opening sketches are
being finished this Friday. The delay was due to our waiting
for similar ideas from Lehninger in order to coordinate a
proper series design. We have now given that up and will go
ahead with yours, and try to adapt his ideas to the design you
like best. You will receive the sketches on Monday.

The finished illustrations are being labeled. Our biology art
editor, Dieter Sussdorf, will review these quickly, indicate
any suggested changes on the overlay, and then sketch any new
illustrations he feels are needed. We will then send these to
you in batches for your approval. The first batch will arrive
in your office about November 26. We expect to finish with
the artwork to you about December 10. The artwork to date has
cost $1301.76 for your artist; probably another $2000.00 for
our artist; and at least $500.00 for our art editor. I doubt
that we can afford to spend much more and stay with the idea
of a $3.95 paperback.

I think the art is superb and no amount of art direction would
have produced the same thing. Our agreement with you was that
we would pay the extra cost of your local artist in lieu of
trying to supply art direction here, and I maintain til doomsday
that this was and is the very best arrangement all around. You
know exactly what you want and I'll bet you reject any suggestions
made by Sussdorf even though we are willing to hire him at this
late date.

Your special request for sample color illustrations will be
attempted, and a couple of drawings in two colors will be sent
by November 26. We cannot make sample color plates. Do you
like the blue in the Gray "Bonding" book (being sent)?

cont.

One Park Avenue
New York, New York 10016
MUrray Hill 9-8850

Dr. James D. Watson   -2-   November 19, 1964

I had intended to follow this with a full scale review of our
attention, in fact devotion, to your manuscript but I think it
shows. I have taken charge of the schedule and will be in touch
with you constantly until all the problems are taken care of and
you are as satisfied as it is humanly possible to manage. Please
bear in mind that you are twice as quick and more intelligent
than 99.99 percent of the people around you, and nothing will
ever come out perfectly for you unless you do it yourself. We
have put out beautiful books in the past and we can do it again.
Neil and I will midwife by candle light if need be.

With best wishes,

William A. Benjamin
President

(See facing page for legend.)

ture," as well as how useful it was, "for professors as well as for students."[23]

One review from the protozoologist Tracy Sonneborn, Watson's former teacher at the University of Indiana, must have been especially gratifying to Watson. Sonneborn wrote:

> *Written and illustrated with brilliant clarity and simplicity, with excitement and enthusiasm, the book is nevertheless uncompromising in its intellectual appeal. The logic of discovery and how theory is advanced by the interplay of experiment and thought dominate the narrative. . . . When a textbook for beginners can so stimulate and excite veterans, it is indeed a most remarkable book.*[24]

"The Molecular Biology of the Gene . . . *eventually sold enough copies to make me almost indifferent to any underpayment as a Harvard professor . . ."* JDW, *Passion for DNA,* p. 120

The book eventually sold more than 100,000 copies and was widely used as the foundation for new courses in molecular biology in the United States. It was also translated into other languages. In style, design, and conception, it was the most original biology textbook yet published and, as such, it had a lasting influence on all subsequent books for students in biology.

(*Facing page*) November 19, 1964, letter from Bill Benjamin, President of W.A. Benjamin, to Watson. He writes, after tallying the costs of the art, "I think the art is superb and no amount of art direction would have produced the same thing. . . . You know exactly what you want and I'll bet you reject any suggestions made by Sussdorf [Benjamin's biology art editor] even though we are willing to hire him at this late date." The last paragraph of the letter shows the publisher's commitment to the book: "I had intended to follow this with a full scale review of our attention, in fact devotion, to your manuscript but I think it shows. . . . Please bear in mind that you are twice as quick and more intelligent than 99.9 percent of the people around you, and nothing will ever come out perfectly for you unless you do it yourself. We have put out beautiful books in the past and we can do it again. Neil and I will midwife by candle light if need be." (Courtesy of the James D. Watson Collection, Cold Spring Harbor Laboratory Archives.)

February 17, 1965

Prof. J. D. Watson
Biology Department
Harvard University
16 Divinity Avenue
Cambridge 38, Massachusetts

Dear Jim:

A couple of notes about your proof changes from Nancy a few days
ago have alarmed me, as your book is going into the crucial paging
stage, and I'd like to take a few moments of your time to discuss
them here, numbering them for future reference.

1. First of all is the matter of printing energy-rich bonds and
    circled Ps in color in the text itself. This can, of course,
    be done; but I wonder whether you will be happy with the
    appearance of a page peppered with spots of color and whether
    such spots might not tend to confuse rather than aid the
    student. A printing difficulty is that of aligning such small
    colored material with the surrounding lines. The ∼ sign and
    the circle are sufficient warning that special bonds and elements
    are involved, even if they are not in color. Please reconsider
    this point, letting us know as soon as possible what your decision
    is. If you truly feel this material in color is essential, we
    must ask that the responsibility for seeing that the proper ones
    are so designated be yours; and you must be sure to mark in the
    page proof everyone you wish to be in color.

2. The next group of corrections have the following problems: (a)
    They are terribly time consuming, and we are already in serious
    schedule difficulties. (b) They are extremely expensive because
    most of the cases must be made by hand, which is charged at a
    rate about 1½ times the original cost of composition. Not only
    must this cost be reflected in the final price of the book, but
    also it is likely to run you AA charges beyond the limits speci-
    fied in the contract. (c) It will mean a lot of extra work for
    you since the marking of every case you want changed would have
    to be your responsibility. With these provisos in mind, let's
    see whether it would be sensible to make these corrections:
    <u>a</u>. If the vertical bars for hydrogen bonds are significant
        (and I can understand that they might be), please mark
        all cases you want changed; neither the printer nor we
        can know which ones are to be so designated.

Numerous letters to Watson from the publisher began to express concern about the mount-
ing costs and the slipping schedule on the book. (*This page*) A February 17, 1965, letter from
David Esner, Executive Editor, asks Watson to reconsider minute changes throughout the
proofs that would have led to expensive corrections. (*Facing page*) A February 18, 1965, letter
from Neil Patterson states that "the company will not pick up any more hotel bills for you.
Costs on the book are away over budget and we must start being as economical as possible."
(Courtesy of the James D. Watson Collection, Cold Spring Harbor Laboratory Archives.
Reprinted with permission of David Esner and Neil Patterson.)

A second edition, with a similar trim size and interior design, also
illustrated by Keith Roberts, was published five years later.[25] This time
it was a proven textbook and not published as part of the teaching

W. A. BENJAMIN, INC.
BOOK PUBLISHERS

February 18, 1965

Dr. James D. Watson
Department of Biology
Harvard University
Cambridge, Massachusetts

Dear Jim,

The president and the controller tell me that the company will
not pick up any more hotel bills for you. Costs on the book are
away over budget now and we must start being as economical as
possible.

I hope you will understand that the final list price of the book is
bound to reflect preparation and production costs and that it is
in your and our best interests to keep these costs to a minimum.

With good wishes,

Neil Patterson
Editor in Chief

Ps.

I hope we can do
your book as a
paperback for
$4.95 or so. Bill and
you have discussed
the notion of
lower royalty, lower price, and
larger volume of sales. What do
you think?

N.

One Park Avenue
New York, New York 10016
MUrray Hill 9-8850

(See facing page for legend.)

monographs series. With two additional chapters, "The Genetic Organization of DNA" and "Embryology on the Molecular Level," it was
longer at 662 pages.

10 August 1965

Mr. Neil Patterson
W.A. Benjamin, Inc.
2465 Broadway
New York, New York 10025

Dear Neil:

I want again to say how pleased I am in my book--now I can't be objective about the text, but as for production, design, etc., you have certainly lived up to your original promises. Let's hope that the general public likes it as well as I do.

I am enclosing a list of people to whom I think the book should be sent. They fall into three categories: 1) molecular biologists or biochemists actively engaged in teaching; 2) people who have read chapters or contributed important figures; 3) molecular biologists whose work plays an important role in the text (e.g. Monod). Since there is probably some overlap with the company's list, someone perhaps should check it.

Again my thanks for all your consideration.

J.D. Watson

JDW:ns
enc.

The book was finally published on July 21, 1965. Watson's letter to Neil Patterson on August 10, 1965, shows that he was happy with the end result. "I want again to say how pleased I am in my book—now I can't be objective about the text, but as for production, design, etc., you have certainly lived up to your original promises. Let's hope that the general public likes it as well as I do." (Courtesy of the James D. Watson Collection, Cold Spring Harbor Laboratory Archives.)

A third edition appeared in 1976[26] and listed previous editions in French, Hungarian, Italian, Japanese, German, Polish, Romanian, Serbo-Croatian, Spanish, and Turkish. The third edition of 739 pages was redesigned in a larger trim size to make it look more like a college introductory biology textbook. Two new chapters were added, "The Essence of Being Eucaryotic" and "The Control of Cell Proliferation."

The fourth edition, published in 1987, was extensively reorganized and written with coauthors Nancy Hopkins, Jeffrey Roberts, Joan Steitz, and Alan Weiner,[27] all former graduate students or postdoctoral fellows of Watson's. The first volume, "General Principles," was published in December 1986 and the second, "Specialized Aspects," in August 1987; there were 1164 pages in all.

The art director and principal artist was George Klatt, assisted by eight contributing artists. There were eight new chapters, much of the new content reflecting the extraordinary fruits of the recombinant

MUSEUM OF COMPARATIVE ZOOLOGY
HARVARD UNIVERSITY
CAMBRIDGE, MASSACHUSETTS 02138

"THE AGASSIZ MUSEUM"

November 1, 1965

Mr. Neil Patterson
Editor in Chief
W.A. Benjamin, Inc.
One Park Avenue
New York, N.Y. 10016

Dear Mr. Patterson:

    I am sorry to be so late in acknowledging receipt of the copy
of James D. Watson's Molecular Biology of the Gene. Before writing
to you I wanted to go through the entire volume which, considering
my crowded schedule, took some time.

    It is my sincere conviction that Watson has done a superb job
in presenting what he promises in the title. What I personally found
most useful is the step by step explanation of the chemical principles
relevant for an understanding of gene structure and gene action. Even
a biologist like myself who has forgotten most of the chemistry he
once knew has no difficulty in following his lucid explanations.
Another point I find quite admirable is the constant stress of that
which we still do not understand. The study of molecular biology is
presented not as finished business but as a dynamic rapidly un-
folding frontier. The final chapters make it clear how important
the new understanding of gene chemistry is for immunology, differen-
tiation and the study of cancer. I congratulate you on being the
publisher of so succesful a volume.

                         Sincerely yours,

                         Ernst Mayr

EM/we

November 1, 1965, letter to Neil Patterson from Ernst Mayr of Harvard. Mayr, a distinguished member of the biology department, knew Watson well. It was he who first showed
the manuscript of *The Double Helix* (then called "Honest Jim") to Harvard University Press.
Watson fell in love with Mayr's daughter Christa, a theme of his second memoir, *Genes, Girls,
and Gamow*. Mayr writes, "It is my sincere conviction that Watson has done a superb job in
presenting what he promises in the title. . . . Even a biologist like myself who has forgotten
most of the chemistry he once knew has no difficulty in following his lucid explanations. . . .
I congratulate you on being the publisher of so successful a volume." (Courtesy of the James
D. Watson Collection, Cold Spring Harbor Laboratory Archives. Reprinted with permission
of Ernst Mayr.)

DNA revolution. The fourth edition was clearly a large-scale collaboration, yet Watson's leadership and input was still critical, as Nancy
Hopkins described:

MEDICAL RESEARCH COUNCIL

Telephone:
Cambridge 48011

LABORATORY OF MOLECULAR BIOLOGY,
UNIVERSITY POSTGRADUATE MEDICAL SCHOOL,
HILLS ROAD,
CAMBRIDGE.

25th October, 1965.

Dr. J. D. Watson,
Biological Laboratories,
Harvard University,
16 Divinity A venue,
Cambridge, Mass. 02138,
U.S.A.

Dear Jim,

Thank you for your interesting, though illegible, letter.
I shall be away from Cambridge during the first two weeks of
December so I hope you will try to arrive before that as it will
be nice to discuss things with you before I go, although I expect
you will still be here when I come back.

Nothing really new to report here. We are intrigued by your
idea about chain initiation but not yet totally convinced.
Perhaps by the time you come here we shall have something more to
tell you.

I enjoyed reading your book very much, although I am not sure
I would have included the last two chapters if I had been writing
it. I also wonder whether I would have put in the first half of
Chapter 2, although I can see your difficulty. I have a number of
small points noted, but they can wait until you come here.
Incidentally, it is very easy to read so I expect you will make a
fortune out of it!

How is the new house going? You should be especially
suspicious of any young lady who offers to help you furnish it!

Your ever,

Francis

Letter to Watson from Francis Crick, October 25, 1965, commenting on *Molecular Biology of the Gene*. "I have enjoyed reading your book very much, although I am not sure I would have included the last two chapters if I had been writing it. I also wonder whether I would have put in the first half of Chapter 2, although I can see your difficulty. I have a number of small points noted, but they can wait until you come here. Incidentally, it is very easy to read so I expect you will make a fortune out of it!" (Courtesy of the James D. Watson Collection, Cold Spring Harbor Laboratory Archives. Reprinted with permission of Francis Crick.)

We always knew his ability to get to the heart of the matter, to see the important point . . . he was almost always right, and had this ability to make the essence of the thing—the apparent—exciting . . . [H]e has this writing style–we called this "Watsonizing" and [we

```
                    State University at Buffalo          528 Highgate Avenue
                                                         Buffalo, New York
                                                         January 6, 1967


        Dr. J. D. Watson
        Department of Biology
        Harvard University
        Cambridge, Massachusetts

        Dear Dr. Watson:
                I am a sophomore majoring in biology
        at the University of Buffalo.  It is now 2
        o'clock in the morning and I am in the midst
        of studying for a final examination in molecu-
        lar biology.  One of the texts which we are now
        using is your Molecular Biology of the Gene.  I
        have read it a number of times and for the past
        few hours I've been reviewing it.
                I'd just like to take this opportunity
        to tell you what a wonderful book it is.  I
        don't think I have ever read a scientific text
        with more life in it than yours.
                Biology is the study or life but
        somehow many authors are successful in "kil-
        ling" it.  Your text is literally overflowing
        with life and vitality.  I am certain that
        anyone reading it would have to say to himself,
        "Wow!  Biology is really a great science!"
                Thanks alot for creating a book which
        is both extremely useful and fascinating.  I
        only wish there were many more like it!

                                    Very truly yours,

                                    Alan R. Zwerner
                                    Alan R. Zwerner
```

Letter from Alan R. Zwerner, an undergraduate student at the State University of New York at Buffalo, January 6, 1967. (Courtesy of the James D. Watson Collection, Cold Spring Harbor Laboratory Archives. Reprinted with the permission of Alan R. Zwerner.) "Biology is the study of life but somehow many authors are successful in 'killing' it. Your text is literally overflowing with life and vitality. I am certain that anyone reading it would have to say to himself, 'Wow! Biology is really a great science!'"

would] just sit there [with a passage] and "Watsonize" it to make it sound like that style. It became a style in which many textbooks are written, due to the extent and the way he formatted Molecular Biology of the Gene, *which was revolutionary when he did it.*[28]

The fifth edition of *Molecular Biology of the Gene* was published in December 2003. Watson's coauthors for this edition were Tania Baker (MIT), Stephen Bell (MIT/HHMI), Alex Gann (Cold Spring Harbor Laboratory), Michael Levine (U.C. Berkeley), and Richard Losick (Harvard).[29]

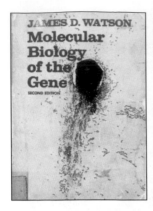
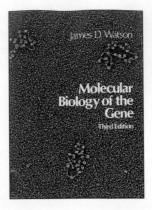
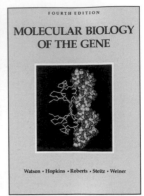

(*Left*) The second edition of *Molecular Biology of the Gene* was published in 1970. Watson writes in the Preface, "The original version of this text might never have been written if I had known how much of my time it would eventually consume. The same is true of this revision. What started out as a summer's part-time task has lasted exactly a year, almost as long as writing the original text." (*Middle*) The third edition, published in 1976, had a larger trim size and was more than 700 pages long. (*Right*) The fourth edition, with four coauthors, appeared originally in two volumes, published in December 1986 and August 1987. Nancy Hopkins, one of Watson's former graduate students and one of the coauthors of the fourth edition, states: "He had this ability to make the essence of the thing—the apparent—exciting." (Reproduced with permission from Benjamin Cummings.)

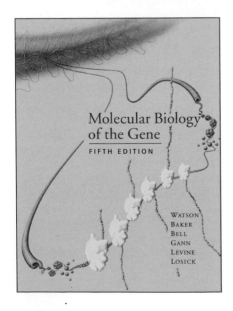

The fifth edition of *Molecular Biology of the Gene* was published in December 2003, in collaboration with Cold Spring Harbor Laboratory Press. There were five coauthors. In planning the fifth edition, the authors, as they note in the Preface, "were all of a mind that much of the organization and scope of the original book should be retained. . . . [M]ore than ever in this genomic era, there seemed a need for a book that explained what genes are and how they work, and this was exactly what *Molecular Biology of the Gene* had originally been designed to do." (Reproduced with permission from Benjamin Cummings.)

Molecular Biology of the Gene was published in a number of languages. (*Top*) Shown here are the first edition: (*left*) Italian translation published in 1967, (*middle*) Turkish translation published in 1968, and (*right*) Russian translation published in 1967. (*Bottom*) The second edition: (*left*) Spanish translation published in 1974 and (*middle*) Polish translation published in 1975. The third edition: (*right*) Italian translation published in 1978. (Photo credit: Phil Renna.)

Notes

1. J.D. Watson. "Manners." Draft manuscript. 2001, 2002. The James D. Watson Collection, Cold Spring Harbor Laboratory Archives.
2. J.D. Watson. "Manners." Draft manuscript. 2001, 2002. The James D. Watson Collection, Cold Spring Harbor Laboratory Archives.

3. S.T. Butler and M. Messel, eds. 1964. *Light and life in the universe.* Shakespeare Head Press, Sydney, Australia.
4. Neil Patterson, private correspondence, January 7, 2002.
5. C. Levinthal. 1965. Editor's Foreword. In *Molecular biology of the gene* (J.D. Watson), p. vii. W.A. Benjamin, Inc., New York.
6. J.D. Watson. "Manners." Draft manuscript. 2001, 2002. The James D. Watson Collection, Cold Spring Harbor Laboratory Archives.
7. J.D. Watson. "Manners." Draft manuscript. 2001, 2002. The James D. Watson Collection, Cold Spring Harbor Laboratory Archives.
8. J.D. Watson. "Manners." Draft manuscript. 2001, 2002. The James D. Watson Collection, Cold Spring Harbor Laboratory Archives.
9. Telephone interview with J.D. Watson, January 10, 2003.
10. Telephone interview with Keith Roberts, December 14, 2001.
11. Telephone interview with Keith Roberts, December 14, 2001.
12. J.D. Watson. 1965. *Molecular biology of the gene*, p. 42. W.A. Benjamin, Inc., New York.
13. J.D. Watson. "Manners." Draft manuscript. 2001, 2002. The James D. Watson Collection, Cold Spring Harbor Laboratory Archives.
14. J.D. Watson. 1965. *Molecular biology of the gene*, p. ix. W.A. Benjamin, Inc., New York.
15. Neil Patterson, private correspondence, January 7, 2002.
16. J.D. Watson. "Manners." Draft manuscript. 2001, 2002. The James D. Watson Collection, Cold Spring Harbor Laboratory Archives.
17. J.D. Watson. 1965. *Molecular biology of the gene*, p. iv. W.A. Benjamin, New York.
18. J.D. Watson. 1965. *Molecular biology of the gene*, p. 1. W.A. Benjamin, New York.
19. G.H. Haggis, D. Michie, A.R. Muir, K.B. Roberts, and P.M.B. Walker. 1964. *Introduction to molecular biology.* Longmans, Green and Co., London.
20. G. Chedd. 1966. A geneticist's view of biology. *Discovery,* March, pp. 53–54.
21. R.D. Hotchkiss. 1966. Grace and logic in biology. *Medical Opinion & Review,* November, pp. 88–89.
22. François Jacob, letter to J.D. Watson, September 20, 1965.
23. André Lwoff, letter to Neil Patterson, October 13, 1965.
24. T.M. Sonneborn. 1965. Teaching Monograph Series (in Book Reviews). *Science* **150:** p. 1282.
25. J.D. Watson. 1970. *Molecular biology of the gene*, 2nd edition (with illus. by K. Roberts). W.A. Benjamin, New York.
26. J.D. Watson. 1976. *Molecular biology of the gene*, 3rd edition (with illus. by K. Roberts). W.A. Benjamin, Menlo Park, California.
27. J.D. Watson, N.H. Hopkins, J.W. Roberts, J.A. Steitz, and A.M. Weiner. 1987. *Molecular biology of the gene*, 4th edition. Benjamin/Cummings, Menlo Park, California.
28. Videotape interview of Nancy Hopkins by Ludmilla Pollock, with Danielle Kovacs, Cambridge, Massachusetts 2001.
29. J.D. Watson, T.A. Baker, S.P. Bell, A. Gann, M. Levine, and R. Losick. 2004. *Molecular biology of the gene*, 5th edition. Pearson/Benjamin Cummings, San Francisco, California (copublished with Cold Spring Harbor Laboratory Press, Cold Spring Harbor, New York).

RECOMBINANT DNA

"There is no substance as important as DNA." Recombinant DNA, Chap. 1

By the early 1980s no textbook of molecular biology, not even Watson's *Molecular Biology of the Gene*, had substantively incorporated the recently developed recombinant DNA technology. Watson and John Tooze had included a scientific background section describing this technology in *The DNA Story*. Teachers told the book's publisher, W.H. Freeman, that this section, if it were modestly expanded, would serve as a much needed supplement to texts (such as the current 1976 edition of Watson's own *Molecular Biology of the Gene*) that had been written before the recombinant DNA revolution had begun to dominate biologists' research.[1] Watson and Tooze set about writing a new book, recruiting David Kurtz, a young researcher at the Cold Spring Harbor Laboratory, who had helped write the scientific background section of *The DNA Story*.

"Our goal was to emphasize the types of experiments that recombinant DNA makes possible . . ." Preface, Recombinant DNA, 1e

The teachers' comments were interpreted by W.H. Freeman in two ways. Some thought instructors were asking for a manual on gene

David Kurtz, 1982, at Cold Spring Harbor. (Courtesy of the Cold Spring Harbor Laboratory Archives and David T. Kurtz.) Kurtz had helped with the "Scientific Background" section of *The DNA Story*, and was recruited by Watson and Tooze to join them in writing *Recombinant DNA*.

cloning. Watson, however, realized that many "how to" manuals would be published, and then become quickly out of date. In his view, the academic community wanted a book that would cover the biological background and the potential of DNA technology.[2] The anti–recombinant DNA lobby had finally lost the battle and scientists could now get on with doing the science, so a text for senior undergraduates and postdocs seemed like a valuable thing to provide.[3]

The resulting book, entitled *Recombinant DNA: A Short Course*, consisted of 18 chapters with 174 illustrations and was 250 pages in length. Watson insisted that the book have the informative chapter titles and descriptive concept heads that characterized *Molecular Biology of the Gene*.[4] Chapter 1, "Establishing the Role of Genes Within Cells," began with a typical Watson sentence: "There is no substance as important as DNA."[5] The first quarter of the book covered traditional DNA biology. But beginning with Chapter 5, "Methods of Creating Recombinant DNA Molecules," the text was devoted primarily to recombinant DNA and gene cloning, with an emphasis on how recombinant DNA technology was impacting biology, medicine, and

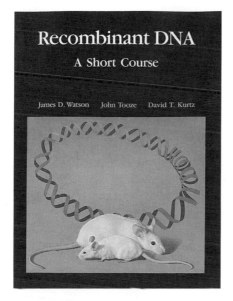

Recombinant DNA: A Short Course, by James D. Watson, John Tooze, and David T. Kurtz, was published in 1982 by W.H. Freeman. The cover illustration by Marvin Mattelson shows a circle of DNA (blue) with a portion in green representing a cloned DNA insert. In the Preface, the authors state their "goal was to emphasize the types of experiments that recombinant DNA makes possible, and to explain some of the important new facts that such experiments have revealed." (Reproduced with permission from W.H. Freeman.)

even the business world ("The Science Used in the Recombinant DNA Industry"). The authors took advantage of the conferences held at Cold Spring Harbor's Banbury Center to ensure that their material was absolutely current.[6] Each chapter was accompanied by a carefully selected reading list and the appendices included a comprehensive list of the known restriction enzymes, their isoschizomers, and recognition sequences well before the mass production of such information by manufacturers.

Watson again turned to the services of *The DNA Story's* George Kelvin as illustrator.[7] The art was rendered in two colors, black and orange, with varying tones that highlighted and differentiated conceptual elements in the illustrations.

Recombinant DNA: A Short Course, was published by W.H. Freeman (Scientific American Books) in 1982. Despite the anticipation by authors and publisher that there might be a limited market for the book, it sold well over 100,000 copies.[8] The reviews were uniformly favorable. Philip Morrison in *Scientific American* said it was "as successful a summary of a discipline in flower as one can find"[9] and the

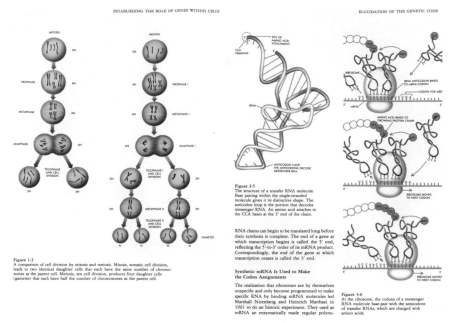

ESTABLISHING THE ROLE OF GENES WITHIN CELLS

ELUCIDATION OF THE GENETIC CODE

Figure 1-3
A comparison of cell division by mitosis and meiosis. Mitosis, somatic cell division, leads to two identical daughter cells that each have the same number of chromosomes as the parent cell. Meiosis, sex cell division, produces four daughter cells (gametes) that each have half the number of chromosomes as the parent cell.

Figure 3-5
The structure of a transfer RNA molecule. Base pairing within the single-stranded molecule gives it its distinctive shape. The anticodon loop is the portion that decodes messenger RNA. An amino acid attaches to the CCA bases at the 3′ end of the chain.

RNA chains can begin to be translated long before their synthesis is complete. The end of a gene at which transcription begins is called the 5′ end, reflecting the 5′-to-3′ order of its mRNA product. Correspondingly, the end of the gene at which transcription ceases is called the 3′ end.

Synthetic mRNA Is Used to Make the Codon Assignments

The realization that ribosomes are by themselves unspecific and only become programmed to make specific RNA by binding mRNA molecules led Marshall Nirenberg and Heinrich Matthaei in 1961 to do an historic experiment. They used as mRNA an enzymatically made regular polynu-

Figure 3-6
At the ribosome, the codons of a messenger RNA molecule base-pair with the anticodons of transfer RNAs, which are charged with amino acids.

The illustrations for the book were the work of George Kelvin, who had drawn the "Visualizing DNA" section for *The DNA Story*. Illustrations were printed in two colors, black and orange, and executed with an airbrush style that gave a three-dimensional look to the images. The figure to the *left* (Fig. 1-3) is an elegant rendering of the processes of mitosis and meioses (cell division). The figure to the *right* shows transfer RNA (Fig. 3-5) and the process of polypeptide synthesis (Fig. 3-6). Watson insisted on high standards for the illustrations in his textbooks. (Reproduced with permission from W.H. Freeman.)

Times Higher Educational Supplement concluded that "[t]his small volume, like Watson's larger works, is likely to become a classic text."[10]

"The first edition sold very well and so if you'd written a good book why not continue it?" JDW INTERVIEW, MARCH 12, 2003

Recombinant DNA technology developed so rapidly that a second edition of the book was soon deemed necessary. Watson recruited Jan Witkowski, Michael Gilman, and Mark Zoller, all then at Cold Spring Harbor Laboratory, as coauthors.[11] It was evident from the very beginning that Watson was not going to do much of the writing himself, but he outlined the book and wrote detailed topic headings that were

Recombinant DNA, second edition, authors. *Left to right:* Mike Gilman, Watson, Mark Zoller, and Jan Witkowski. (Photo courtesy of Margot Bennett.) All were at Cold Spring Harbor Laboratory during the time the second edition was being written.

modified as the manuscript was written. Much of the basic biology of DNA was retained, but the second edition also included the application of DNA technology in industry, human genetics, and gene therapy, and the basic principles employed in deciphering the human genome sequence.

Now with 23 chapters, the second edition had increased to 626 pages and 369 four-color illustrations. Two distinguishing features of this edition, which was published in 1992, were its use of real experiments to illustrate important biological phenomena and its inclusion of exciting research at the cutting edge of biology. Like its predecessor, it was enormously successful, realizing sales of more than 100,000 copies.

A third edition of *Recombinant DNA*, now subtitled "Genes and Genomes," is under way.

The second edition of *Recombinant DNA* was published in 1992 by W.H. Freeman. The cover illustration was again by Marvin Mattelson and symbolized key elements in the book: the DNA double helix and blocks of double-stranded DNA fragments synthesized by the polymerase chain reaction. The coat colors of the mice running down the helix change from albino to chimeric to agouti, color changes that show in mice in which genetic engineering has been used to knock out a specific gene. Prior to becoming a now-prominent portrait painter, Mattelson was an award-winning illustrator, commissioned to paint covers for magazines and book covers. (Reproduced with permission from W.H. Freeman.)

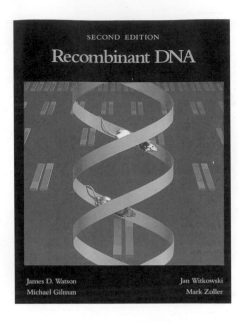

Book celebrations for the publication of the second edition were held at New York City's elegant and upscale French restaurant, Lutèce (*left*), and at Blackford Bar at Cold Spring Harbor Laboratory (*right*, flyer). (*Left*, Courtesy of Readio.com; photo credit: Wanda McCormick. *Right*, Courtesy of the James D. Watson Collection, Cold Spring Harbor Laboratory Archives. Cartoon reprinted with permission of S. Harris.)

Translations of the second edition of *Recombinant DNA*. *Clockwise from upper left:* the Japanese translation, the German translation, the French translation, and the Italian translation. (Photo credit: Miriam Chua.)

Notes

1. J.D. Watson, J. Tooze, and D.T. Kurtz. 1982. Preface. In *Recombinant DNA: A short course*, p. xv. Scientific American Books, New York.
2. Interview with David Kurtz, March 8, 2003.
3. Interview with John Tooze, March 10, 2003.
4. Interview with David Kurtz, March 8, 2003.
5. J.D. Watson, J. Tooze, and D.T. Kurtz. 1982. *Recombinant DNA: A short course*. Scientific American Books, New York.
6. Interview with David Kurtz, March 8, 2003.
7. Interview with David Kurtz, March 8, 2003.
8. Interview with David Kurtz, March 8, 2003.
9. P. Morrison. 1984. Books. *Sci. Am.* **250:** 31, March.
10. *Times Higher Educational Supplement,* quoted from W.H. Freeman's advertising copy.
11. J.D. Watson, M. Gilman, J. Witkowski, and M. Zoller. 1992. *Recombinant DNA,* 2nd edition, p. xiv. Scientific American Books, New York.

MOLECULAR BIOLOGY OF THE CELL

"This is a large book, and it has been a long time in gestation—three times longer than an elephant, five times longer than a whale." PREFACE, *MBOC*, P. V

Before *Molecular Biology of the Gene*, biochemistry had failed to convey the importance of genes as the master blueprints for cellular metabolism. Cell biology textbooks in the 1960s and 1970s were mired in description, with little integration of structure and function. Watson was increasingly aware of this weakness and had added aspects of cell biology to the third edition of *Molecular Biology of the Gene*,[1] but he recognized that a proper treatment of modern cell biology would require a book of its own.

"Gavin was like a character in a book, a most unusual man." JDW
IN *JAMES WATSON: HOW DO YOU START A BOOK*—HEATHER RAFF

After successfully launching Watson's *Molecular Biology of the Gene* with W.A. Benjamin, Neil Patterson eventually began his own company, Neil Patterson Publishers, in partnership with a New York–based, liberal arts publisher Gavin Borden, whose company, Garland Publishing, had published the 63-volume *James Joyce Archive*. In the late

Author meeting, Nugent Terrace, St. John's Wood, London. *Left to right:* Julian Lewis, Keith Roberts, and Gavin Borden, publisher, with cigar. Gavin's spirit and style were crucial in the formation of the author team and the working relationships that developed over the years as *Molecular Biology of the Cell* was written. (Photo courtesy of Libby Borden.)

1970s, Borden was seeking entrée into the world of college biology textbooks, attracted by their profit potential.[2] Patterson approached Watson about writing an introductory textbook in biology, but emerged from his talks with Watson instead with an idea for an interesting account of how cells work at the molecular level.[3] Watson signed a contract for this book as the first member of a not-yet-named multi-author team.

Soon, however, Patterson departed to run W.H. Freeman and the cell biology book was left entirely in Gavin Borden's hands. Watson liked Borden immediately. He was a man of spirit and style, with a capacity for diverse and deep friendships,[4] someone born to privilege who moved in many different social worlds, was interested in people, and loved literature and books.[5]

In the late 1970s, multiauthored college textbooks were rare. But with his many other commitments, Watson never considered writing

Molecular Biology of the Cell on his own. So he and Borden began assembling a team of authors. Keith Roberts was recruited for his expertise in plant biology and as the originator of yet another set of novel, essential illustrations. Watson knew that Martin Raff at University College, London, was thinking and writing about things other than his own work,[6] and Borden approached Raff. Raff initially declined, but then agreed to join a discussion of the project.[7] Joe Sambrook, a virologist and cell biologist at Cold Spring Harbor, another skilled writer, completed an initial cast of anticipated authors.

The meeting in London changed Raff's mind about the project:

> *Jim's vision was that there was a need to change the way people thought about and taught cell biology. . . . It would accelerate and catalyze the process of integrating the old-fashioned view of cell biology that was largely microscopy-based, with modern cell and molecular biology that was changing the way one understood cells.[8]*

Also, Watson's belief that four or five authors would only need to write one chapter and edit material acquired from established experts made it sound like a two-year project and too good to turn down.[9]

In the summer of 1978 the authors convened at Watson's home on Martha's Vineyard. They included Bruce Alberts from the University of California, San Francisco, who, though reluctant to get involved, had been persuaded to replace Sambrook, who had withdrawn from the project, and help edit the commissioned chapters.[10] The experience of working together was creative and enjoyable and they were not expecting to finish the book then.[11]

The next summer at Fort Hill near Cold Spring Harbor was much harder. "It was a very hard summer," according to Alberts, "It was hot as anything, and we worked all the time, and we had conflicts with people."[12] Raff and Alberts were learning that textbook writing is very different from writing papers. They also realized that the book was going to take much longer than anticipated and that they were going to have to write most of it themselves.[13] Other potential authors were considered but found wanting until a very nice draft chapter on development was received from Julian Lewis; he was promptly recruited as

Letter to Watson from Bruce Alberts, March 14, 1978. (Courtesy of the James D. Watson Collection, Cold Spring Harbor Laboratory Archives. Reprinted with permission of Bruce Alberts.) Alberts writes: "I am still mulling over your attractive and interesting offer to be a co-author on a new cell biology book . . . I received several cell biology books in the mail from the publisher which I read over this weekend. I agree that they are pretty awful . . . [t]he student is faced with a stream of continuous writing with no sharp definition into conceptual points to be understood. Organization into one or two page sections in each of which some major idea is explained would seem to be essential. This was beautifully done in your 'Molecular Biology of the Gene' . . . ."

a permanent author. Things improved and the author team gradually became deeply committed to producing a book.[14, 15]

Borden was always in the background, inspiring a sense of camaraderie among the authors.[16] The authors thought initially that he was independently wealthy, but in fact he had borrowed a lot of money to get the book going and was taking a huge risk.[17] Bright, stylish, intellectually alert, and emotionally encouraging, Borden was not the ordinary textbook publisher.[18] The authors also all had huge respect for Watson, recognizing that without him the project would have never started. But there was never any sense that he was the senior author, making all the decisions. According to Bruce Alberts, "When *we* thought something was good *he* thought it was good. He's got a great

UNIVERSITY OF CALIFORNIA, SAN FRANCISCO

BERKELEY · DAVIS · IRVINE · LOS ANGELES · RIVERSIDE · SAN DIEGO · SAN FRANCISCO SANTA BARBARA · SANTA CRUZ

SCHOOL OF MEDICINE   SAN FRANCISCO, CALIFORNIA 94143
DEPARTMENT OF BIOCHEMISTRY AND BIOPHYSICS (415) 666-4324

February 22, 1979

Mr Gavin Borden
Garland Publishing, Inc.
545 Madison Avenue
New York, New York 10022

Dear Gavin:

I am replying to your note of February 5, in which you enclosed the
comments of Dan Schiller about Martin and my chapters 5 and 26. Of
course, for me, Martin's chapter is easiest to discuss. I think it
needs considerable trimming towards the end where he tries to explain
things which are really not at all yet clear. However, I know everyone
here found his chapter most useful for teaching immunology even in
draft, and I think that it would be a mistake to reduce it to ten book
pages or so a la Dyson. If the book can accommodate it, reducing the
text by about 25% (Schiller's possibility 2) would be optimal. Cutting
somewhat more than this might be possible, since the material at the end
should be highly condensed.

With regard to my chapter, Schiller's comments mainly reflect upon the
general attitude that we have had of trying to keep all of the presentation
interesting. This means that somehow we have to avoid "slogging through
the basic biochemistry". During Martin and my discussions with Jim, we
basically felt that we need to find a new format in which to present the
kind of information which Schiller finds to be missing without boring
the reader. It seems to me that to do a lot of this in the context of
history in Chapter 3 would at least be worth a try. Perhaps Jim and I should
work together on this this summer.

Another factor, of which Schiller was not aware, is that we had made a
decision to put a lot of the "boring" basic biochemistry into large one
or two page figures, which Keith is to draw and which will then be
annotated with extensive headings. Perhaps this is a mistake, but we
might wait to see how the one in progress on nucleic acids turns out,
for example, before deciding. Thus, an option would be to add additional
figures of this type in which we introduce carbohydrates, lipids, etc.
as chemical entities. The reason why we originally chose this strategy
was to get such basically boring factual material out of the text, so
that it would not interrupt the flow of ideas. I think you should
discuss this whole problem with Jim in detail, as soon as possible.

A final note is that I have always anticipated that we would have the
kind of problems which Schiller raises, and that these would delay our
getting the final book in acceptable form. I felt last summer (and
still feel), that there is no way we are going to be able to manage it
all this summer. My aim is to have a real masterpiece when this is done,
and I do not see why we should hurry at the inevitable expense of quality.

Best regards,

Bruce M. Alberts

Letter to publisher Gavin Borden from Bruce Alberts, February 22, 1979. (Courtesy of the
James D. Watson Collection, Cold Spring Harbor Laboratory Archives. Reprinted with permission of Bruce Alberts.) Alberts is now fully on board, and taking the lead, discussing details
of chapters being reviewed by others. He notes that "we . . . made a decision to put a lot of
the 'boring' basic biochemistry into large one or two page figures, which Keith is to draw and
which will then be annotated with extensive headings. . . . The reason why we originally chose
this strategy was to get such basically boring factual material out of the text, so that it would
not interrupt the flow of ideas." The letter concludes: "My aim is to have a real masterpiece
when this is done, and I do not see why we should hurry at the inevitable expense of quality."

An early author meeting for the first edition of *Molecular Biology of the Cell* at Fort Hill, Cold Spring Harbor, circa 1979. *Left to right:* Gavin Borden (the publisher), Watson, Bruce Alberts, and Martin Raff. Watson wrote in a letter to Keith Porter in January, 1979, regarding the publisher (Garland), which was started by and still effectively owned by Gavin Borden, "He is a friend of Bob Worth, and more than knows that much, much money will be needed to produce the super illustrated and clearly written text which has been so long overdue." (Photo courtesy of Keith Roberts.)

sense for that sort of thing and when we finally got it right he was really enthusiastic."[19] When Dennis Bray was recruited, the authors at last felt they could produce something significant.[20]

In subsequent summers, the writing and discussions moved to various locales, and in 1982 Borden leased a roomy house for the authors in St. John's Wood, London, near Abbey Road, where a Xerox machine and computers were installed.[21] Many interesting people came through the house all the time, so it was like an ongoing graduate seminar.[22]

". . . we have attempted to write the book so that even a stranger to biology could follow it . . ." PREFACE, *MBOC,* P. V

After five years in preparation, *Molecular Biology of the Cell* was finally ready to be printed. Like *Molecular Biology of the Gene* and

Recombinant DNA, Molecular Biology of the Cell contained multiple primary descriptive headings as well as one-sentence-style subheadings. The book had other innovative features, such as multiple time lines showing key historical milestones in cell biology. Keith Roberts' illustrations were profuse and impeccably designed.

Many experts who had reviewed the chapters said it was totally inappropriate for an undergraduate textbook because it was too conceptual, with too many hypothetical models. Raff thought there was a good chance the book would not succeed. But Watson was constant in his conviction that ". . . this is just what's needed. People said the same things about MBG." And he was right.[23]

The reviews vindicated Watson's sense of a void in the market. Hewson Swift, the noted biologist from the University of Chicago, recognized this immediately:

> *A lot of subjects in biology are becoming harder and harder to teach, and cell biology is no exception. This book . . . is bound to be of considerable assistance. . . . Its influence on what is taught in cell biology courses is likely to be substantial.*[24]

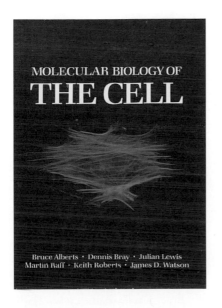

The first edition of *Molecular Biology of the Cell* came out in 1983. The cover shows a stylized cell. Authors were listed in alphabetical order. (Reproduced with permission from Taylor & Francis Group. Photo credit: Phil Renna.)

Department of Biology

WASHINGTON
UNIVERSITY
IN ST LOUIS

Dear Bruce,

I want to be one of the first in the chorus to congratulate you on the best ~~book~~ textbook that has ever been produced. Even after seeing Chapter 8 alone, John and I sent our advance royalty on a cell biology text back to Benjamin/Cummings Inc. There was/is no point in even getting started: you've done it all. The students in my cell biology course are uniformly enthusiastic. Perhaps the best news I can impart is the following. The man who teaches our <u>introductory</u> <u>course</u> (350 students) wants to adopt it for next year, and the man who organizes our cell biology course at the <u>medical school</u> (100 students) wants to adopt it for next year. In other words, you've managed the impossible. I've read about 1/3 of it now and wouldn't change a line. Thanks so much for what was clearly a heroic effort; may you now bask in its glory.

Ursula Goodenough

Washington University
Campus Box 1137
St. Louis, Mo. 63130

Letter to Bruce Alberts from Ursula Goodenough in 1983. (Courtesy of the James D. Watson Collection, Cold Spring Harbor Laboratory Archives. Reprinted with permission from Ursula Goodenough.) "I want to be one of the first in the chorus to congratulate you on the best textbook that has ever been produced. Even after seeing Chapter 8 alone, John [Heuser] and I sent our advance royalty on a cell biology text back to Benjamin/Cummings Inc. There was/is no point in even getting started: you've done it all. The students in my cell biology class are uniformly enthusiastic." Goodenough, herself, had published a book, *Genetics*, in 1974 with Holt, Rinehart and Winston. The first edition was written with Robert Paul Levine while she was a postdoc at Harvard and is recognized as a classic in the field.

The publication of the second edition of *Molecular Biology of the Cell* was celebrated at the aquarium in San Francisco. *Left to right:* Keith Roberts, Bruce Alberts, Watson, Julian Lewis, and Martin Raff. (Photo courtesy of Libby Borden.)

(*Left*) Gavin Borden and (*right*) Libby Borden, summer 1991. Gavin died prematurely of salivary gland cancer in December 1991 at the age of 51. In his honor, Cold Spring Harbor Laboratory established, in 1995, the Gavin Borden Visiting Fellowship to pay tribute to the charismatic publisher and founder of Garland. Each year the Lab's graduate students choose an inspiring scientist to speak to students and staff during a two-day stay at the Laboratory. (Photos courtesy of Libby Borden.)

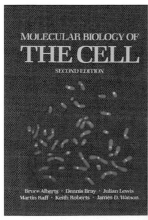
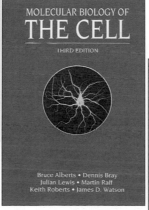

Left to right: The second edition (1989), third edition (1994), and fourth edition (2002) of *Molecular Biology of the Cell.* Each cover was in a different color and featured an image pertinent to cell biology. (Reproduced with permission from Taylor & Francis Group.)

It was heartily recommended for classroom use,[25] and thought certain to make a major mark upon students, instructors, and research biologists alike.[26]

Like all successful textbooks, *Molecular Biology of the Cell* has been frequently revised. Watson participated in the writing and organization of all but the fourth edition,[27] published in 2002. *Molecular Biology of the Cell* has remained innovative, beautiful to look at, hugely successful in financial and educational terms, and the most influential cell biology textbook of its time.

Notes

1. Heather Raff, personal communication of unpublished material.
2. Interview with Libby Borden, May 12, 2003.
3. Interview with Neil Patterson, March 17, 2003.
4. Heather Raff, personal communication of unpublished material.
5. Interview with James D.Watson, March 12, 2003.
6. Heather Raff, personal communication of unpublished material.
7. Interview with Martin Raff, April 24, 2003.
8. Interview with Martin Raff, April 24, 2003.
9. Interview with Martin Raff, April 24, 2003.
10. Interview with Bruce Alberts, May 2, 2003.
11. Interview with Bruce Alberts, May 2, 2003.
12. Interview with Bruce Alberts, May 2, 2003.
13. Interview with Bruce Alberts, May 2, 2003.
14. Interview with Bruce Alberts, May 2, 2003.
15. Interview with Heather Raff, March 13, 2003. Writing under the name Heather Burton, Heather Raff documented the writing of *Molecular Biology of the Cell* shortly after Borden's untimely death in 1991. "It was a very moving time," she related, "I went to Cold Spring Harbor and talked to Jim, and I went to New York to talk to Libby [Borden, Gavin's former wife]. I also talked to the other authors, including those in England, and from a completely layman's point of view I wrote about those dynamics." A piece entitled *"Still in Process": Collaborative Authorship in a Twentieth Century Biomedical Textbook* is published [*Can. Bull. Med. Hist.* **12:** 373–384, 1995]. A more extensive piece on the same topic and based on extensive interviews with all the authors of *Molecular Biology of the Cell* is currently unpublished.
16. Interview with Bruce Alberts, May 2, 2003.
17. Interview with Bruce Alberts, May 2, 2003.
18. Interview with Neil Patterson, March 17, 2003.

19. Interview with Bruce Alberts, May 2, 2003.

20. Interview with Bruce Alberts, May 2, 2003.

21. Interview with Bruce Alberts, May 2, 2003.

22. Interview with Heather Raff, March 13, 2003.

23. Interview with Martin Raff, April 24, 2003.

24. H. Swift. 1984. *Am. Sci.* **72:** 286, May/June.

25. W.H. Massover. 1983. Cell biology for students. *Science* **220** 856–857, May 20.

26. M.E. Beard. 1984. Expert and expertly edited: This cell biology text shouldn't be missed. *BioScience* **34:** 449, July/August.

27. Four editions of *Molecular Biology of the Cell* have been published:
    B. Alberts, D. Bray, J. Lewis, M. Raff, K. Roberts, and J.D. Watson. 1983. *Molecular biology of the cell.* Garland Publishing, Inc., New York & London.
    B. Alberts, D. Bray, J. Lewis, M. Raff, K. Roberts and J.D. Watson. 1989. *Molecular biology of the cell,* 2nd edition. Garland Publishing, Inc., New York & London.
    B. Alberts, D. Bray, J. Lewis, M. Raff, K. Roberts, and J.D. Watson. 1994. *Molecular biology of the cell,* 3rd edition. Garland Publishing (Taylor & Francis Group), New York.
    B. Alberts, A. Johnson, J. Lewis, M. Raff, K. Roberts, and P. Walter. 2002. *Molecular biology of the cell,* 4th edition. Garland Science (Taylor & Francis Group), New York.

CODA

"Never do anything that bores you." JDW, PASSION FOR DNA, P. 125

James Watson is not alone among many celebrated scientists who have had writing in their blood, creating essays and books for the general public rather than for other scientists. With *The Double Helix*, James Watson placed himself among a handful of scientist–authors, such as Richard Feynman, Stephen Hawking, and Lewis Thomas, who have achieved both popular acclaim and extraordinary sales success. Certainly, few scientific topics have captured the interest and attention of the general public as much as DNA has. But Watson has told the tale of DNA with exceptional skill, raising DNA itself to iconic status.

Even without his textbooks, which have had unrivaled educational influence and commercial success, *The Double Helix* alone would have established Watson's reputation: It is the only book about science among the best 100 nonfiction works selected in a poll by the Modern Library,[1] and it has ". . . revolutionized the way science would be portrayed in nonfiction books thereafter,"[2] according to Matt Ridley. In his Foreword to *Inspiring Science*, Ridley points out:

> *Not only do today's science writers depict their characters as human beings . . . they take them by the hand to embark on a tour of discovery. They do what Watson did: show them the ignorance that came first, not the established facts that came later. They convey the excitement of chipping away at mystery, rather than compiling knowledge.[3]*

Watson, speaking at a book signing at the Book Revue, Huntington, New York. (Courtesy of the James D. Watson Collection, Cold Spring Harbor Laboratory Archives.) The Book Revue has remained a haven for authors and bibliophiles of the Cold Spring Harbor community and surrounds for more than a quarter century, thanks to the kind hospitality of owners Robert and Richard Klein.

Watson's reputation as a writer also derives from his willingness to "tell it like it is." The geneticist and science historian Elof Carlson has commented on Watson's courage in "presenting history as [he] experienced it rather than as a fraudulent fantasy of progress."[4] Such candor derives from a strong ego fortified by Watson's celebrity status and a well-developed sense of moral integrity inculcated early in life that makes it acceptable to "call crap, crap."[5] Asked if he had avoided writing about a subject or person out of a sense of propriety, Watson's answer was a simple "no."[6] And this honesty also applies to himself. How many autobiographers with a place as secure in the history of sci-

Book signing at the University of Alabama, Birmingham, November 15, 1988. (Courtesy of the James D. Watson Collection, Cold Spring Harbor Laboratory Archives.)

ence as Watson's would risk the personal revelations in *Genes, Girls, and Gamow?*

Writing is fundamental to history, describing who we are and what we do, and in this respect Jim Watson has been a professor in the strict scholarly sense of the word. He has been a promoter of many scientific enterprises and of many areas of modern molecular biology, as well as a public figure who has provoked scientists, politicians, and society at large to think more deeply about the controversial issues of socio-scientific importance of the past 50 years. And his contributions to education—with the *Molecular Biology of the Gene* regarded as the most important textual contribution to the discipline of molecular biology—are a rich legacy to the classrooms where future generations of scientists are being trained and inspired. The qualities that charac-

James D. Watson, professor, promoter, provocateur, with a model of the molecule that made him so famous. (Courtesy of the Cold Spring Harbor Laboratory Archives. Photo credit: Sue Lauter.)

terize Jim Watson's writings—the candor, forthrightness, and rectitude that may earn him scathing reviews—validate the truth of the ironic title given him on a mountainside more than 50 years ago—"Honest Jim."

Notes

1. Random House Adult Trade Publishing Group's *Modern Library* reader's poll for the best nonfiction published in the the English language since 1900 opened on April 29, 1999, and closed on September 30, 1999, with a total of 194,829 votes cast. See http://www.randomhouse.com/modernlibrary/100bestnonfiction.html.
2. M. Ridley. 2003. Foreword. In *Inspiring science: Jim Watson and the age of DNA*, p. xvi. Cold Spring Harbor Laboratory Press, Cold Spring Harbor, New York.
3. M. Ridley. 2003. Foreword. In *Inspiring science: Jim Watson and the age of DNA*, p. xvii. Cold Spring Harbor Laboratory Press, Cold Spring Harbor, New York.
4. Elof Carlson, letter to James D. Watson, January 1, 1968.
5. A paraphrase of Watson's famous quote from *A Passion for DNA* (p. 5): "You were never held back by manners, and crap was best called crap. Offending somebody was always preferable to avoiding the truth, though such bluntness did not make me a social success with most of my classmates."
6. Interview with James D. Watson, February 9, 2002.

BIBLIOGRAPHY—
JAMES D. WATSON[1]

Watson J.D. 1950. The properties of X-ray-inactivated bacteriophage. I. Inactivation by direct effect. *J. Bacteriol.* **60:** 697–718.

Maaløe O. and Watson J.D. 1951. The transfer of radioactive phosphorous from parental to progeny phage. *Proc. Natl. Acad. Sci.* **37:** 507–513.

Watson J.D. 1952. The properties of X-ray-inactivated bacteriophage. II. Inactivation of indirect effects. *J. Bacteriol.* **63:** 473–485.

Watson J.D. and Maaløe O. 1953. Nucleic acid transfer from parental to progeny bacteriophage. *Biochim. Biophys. Acta* **10:** 432–442.

Watson J.D. and Hayes W. 1953. Genetic exchange in *Escherichia coli* K12: Evidence for three linkage groups. *Proc. Natl. Acad. Sci.* **39:** 416–426.

Ephrussi B., Leopold U., Watson J.D., and Weigle J. 1953. Terminology in bacterial genetics. *Nature* **171:** 701.

Watson J.D. and Crick F.H.C. 1953. A structure for deoxyribose nucleic acid. *Nature* **171:** 737–738.

Watson J.D. and Crick F.H.C. 1953. Genetic implications of the structure of deoxyribonucleic acid. *Nature* **171:** 964–967.

Watson J.D. and Crick F.H.C. 1953. The structure of DNA. *Cold Spring Harbor Symp. Quant. Biol.* **18:** 123–131.

Crick F.H.C. and Watson J.D. 1954. The complementary structure of deoxyribonucleic acid. *Proc. Roy. Soc. A* **223:** 80–96.

Watson J.D. 1954. The structure of tobacco mosaic virus. I. X-ray evidence of a helical arrangement of sub-units around the longitudinal axis. *Biochim. Biophys. Acta* **13:** 10–19.

Rich A. and Watson J.D. 1954. Some relations between DNA and RNA. *Proc. Natl. Acad. Sci.* **40:** 759–764.

Rich A. and Watson J.D. 1954. Physical studies on ribonucleic acid. *Nature* **173:** 995–996.

[1]Major works of J.D. Watson, including first editions; reprinted, with permission, from *Inspiring science: Jim Watson and the age of DNA* (ed. J. Inglis, J. Sambrook, and J. Witkowski), pp. 477–481. Cold Spring Harbor Laboratory Press, Cold Spring Harbor, New York.

(*Facing page, top*) Chapter 1, "The Mendelian View of the World." (*Facing page, bottom*) The second page contains a statement that is the premise of the book: "evolutionary theory further affects our thinking by suggesting that the basic principles of the living state are the same in all living forms." (*This page*) A heavily edited earlier version of the statement, "Nonetheless Evolutionary theory profoundly affects our thinking by suggesting that the basic principles of the living state will be the same in living forms," shows that Watson was seeking the clearest statement of this idea. (All courtesy of the James D. Watson Collection, Cold Spring Harbor Laboratory Archives.)

Crick F.H.C. and Watson J.D. 1955. The configuration of the nucleic acids. *Inst. Lombardo Sci. Lett.* **89:** 52–66.

Watson J.D. 1955. Biological consequences of the complementary structure of DNA. *J. Cell. Comp. Physiol.* **45:** 109–118.

Crick F.H.C. and Watson J.D. 1956. The structure of small viruses. *Nature* **177:** 473–475.

Watson J.D. 1957. X-ray studies on RNA and the synthetic polyribonucleotides. In *The chemical basis of heredity* (ed. W.D. McElroy and B. Glass), pp. 552–556. Johns Hopkins Press, Baltimore, Maryland.

Crick F.H.C. and Watson J.D. 1957. Virus structure: General principles. In *Ciba Foundation Symposium on the nature of viruses* (ed. G.E.W. Wolstenholme and E.C.P. Millar), pp. 5–13. Little, Brown, Boston, Massachusetts.

Koshland Jr., D.E., Simmons N.S., and Watson J.D. 1958. Absence of phosphotriester linkages in tobacco mosaic virus *J. Am. Chem. Soc.* **80:** 105–107.

Tissières A. and Watson J.D. 1958. Ribonucleoprotein particles from *Escherichia coli. Nature* 182: 778-780.

Nomura M. and Watson J.D. 1959. Ribonucleoprotein particles with chloromycetin-inhibited *Escherichia coli. J. Mol. Biol.* **1:** 204–217.

Tissières A., Watson J.D., Schlessinger D., and Hollingworth B.R. 1959. Ribonucleoprotein particles from *Escherichia coli. J. Mol. Biol.* **1:** 221–233.

Watson J.D. and Littlefield J.W. 1960. Some properties of DNA from Shope papilloma virus *J. Mol. Biol.* **2:** 161–165.

Rich A., Davies D.R., Crick F.H.C., and Watson J.D. 1961. The molecular structure of polyadenylic acid *J. Mol. Biol.* **3:** 71–86.

Gros F., Hiatt H., Gilbert W., Kurland C.G., Risebrough R.W., and Watson J.D. 1961. Unstable ribonucleic acid revealed by pulse labeling of *E. coli. Nature* **190:** 581–584.

Gros F., Gilbert W., Hiatt H., Attardi G., Spahr P.F., and Watson J.D. 1962. Molecular and biological characterization of messenger RNA. *Cold Spring Harbor Symp. Quant. Biol.* **26:** 111–132.

Risebrough R.W., Tissières A., and Watson J.D. 1962. Messenger RNA attachment to active ribosomes. *Proc. Natl. Acad. Sci.* **48:** 430–436.

Kurland C.G., Nomura M., and Watson J.D. 1962. The physical properties of chloromycetin particles. *J. Mol. Biol.* **4:** 388–394.

Tissières A. and Watson J.D. 1962. Breakdown of messenger RNA during in-vitro amino acid incorporation into proteins. *Proc. Natl. Acad. Sci.* **48:** 1061–1069.

Watson J.D. 1963. Involvement of RNA in the synthesis of proteins. In *Les Prix Nobel en 1962*, pp. 155–178. Nobel Foundation, Stockholm, Sweden.

Watson J.D. 1963. Involvement of RNA in the synthesis of proteins (adapted from Nobel Lecture, December 1962). *Science* **140:** 17–26.

Watson J.D. 1964. The synthesis of proteins upon ribosomes. *Bull. Soc. Chim. Biol.* **46:** 1399–1425.

Watson J.D. 1964. The replication of living molecules. In *Light and life in the universe* (ed. S.T. Butler and H. Messel), pp. 295–340. Shakespeare Head Press, Sydney, Australia.

Watson J.D. 1965. *Molecular biology of the gene.* W.A. Benjamin, New York.

Cairns J., Stent G.S., and Watson J.D., eds. 1966. *Phage and the origins of molecular biology.* Cold Spring Harbor Laboratory of Quantitative Biology, Cold Spring Harbor, New York.

Watson J.D. 1966. Growing up in the phage group. In *Phage and the origins of molecular biology* (ed. J. Cairns et al.), pp. 239–245. Cold Spring Harbor Laboratory of Quantitative Biology, Cold Spring Harbor, New York.

Watson J.D. 1966. Life's molecules take shape. *New Sci.* **32:** 424, 425, 428.

Gussin G.N., Capecchi M.R., Adams J.M., Argetsinger J.E., Tooze J., Weber K., and Watson J.D. 1967. Protein synthesis directed by RNA phage messengers. *Cold Spring Harbor Symp. Quant. Biol.* **31:** 257–271.

Watson J.D. 1968. *The double helix: A personal account of the discovery of the structure of DNA.* Atheneum, New York.

Eigner J., Watson J.D., Haselkorn R., Signer E., Fraser D., and Echols H. 1968. Letter: Boycott Chicago! *Science* **162:** 511.

Watson J.D. 1969. Looking after molecular biologists. Director's Report in the Annual Report of Cold Spring Harbor Laboratory.

Watson J.D. 1969. Letter: DNA helix. *Science* **164:** 1539.

Watson J.D. 1970. Communicating the frontiers of science. Director's Report in the Annual Report of Cold Spring Harbor Laboratory.

Watson J.D. 1971. Moving toward the clonal man: Is this what we want? *Atlantic Monthly* **227:** 50–53.

Watson J.D. 1971. The conquest of cancer—How to use money and resources wisely? Director's Report in the Annual Report of Cold Spring Harbor Laboratory.

Watson J.D. 1972. The cancer conquerors. Who should get all that new money? *The New Republic* **166:** 17–21.

Watson J.D. 1972. Origin of concatemeric T7 DNA. *Nat. New Biol.* **239:** 197–201.

Watson J.D. 1972. On being an entrepreneur of science. Director's Report in the Annual Report of Cold Spring Harbor Laboratory.

Watson J.D. 1973. Escalating the war on cancer. *Science Year: A World Book Science Annual,* pp. 24–32.

Watson J.D. 1973. When worlds collide: Research and know-nothingism. *The New York Times Op-Ed,* March 22.

Watson J.D. 1973. Tumor viruses—A route to Mt. Everest of cancer. Director's Report in the Annual Report of Cold Spring Harbor Laboratory.

Berg P., Baltimore D., Boyer H.W., Cohen S.N. , Davis R.W., Hogness D.S., Nathans D., Roblin R., Watson J.D., Weissman S., and Zinder N.D. 1974. Letter: Potential biohazards of recombinant DNA molecules. *Science* **185:** 303.

Watson J.D. 1974. Getting realistic about cancer. Director's Report in the Annual Report of Cold Spring Harbor Laboratory.

Wason J.D. 1975. The dissemination of unpublished information. In *Frontiers of knowledge: The Frank Nelson Doubleday Lectures,* pp. 158–175. Doubleday, New York.

Watson J.D. 1975. Have molecular geneticists become intellectually passé? Director's Report in the Annual Report of Cold Spring Harbor Laboratory.

Watson J.D. 1976. A massive miscalculation—The "dangers" of recombinant DNA. Director's Report in the Annual Report of Cold Spring Harbor Laboratory.

Watson J.D. 1977. An imaginary monster. *Bull. At. Sci.* **33:** 12–13.

Watson J.D. 1977. In defense of DNA. *New Republic* **170:** 11–14.

Watson J.D. 1977. Molecular biologists and political realities. Director's Report in the Annual Report of Cold Spring Harbor Laboratory.

Watson J.D. 1978. Trying to bury Asilomar. *Clin. Res.* **26:** 113–115.

Watson J.D. 1978. The case for expanding research into DNA. *N. Z. Vet. J.* **26:** 182.

Watson J.D. 1978. The Nobelist vs the film star. *The Washington Post,* Sunday, May 14. D1–D2.

Watson J.D. 1978. The Ninth Feodor Lynen Lecture: In further defense of DNA. *Miami Winter Symp.* **15:** 1–12.

Watson J.D. 1978. Standing up for recombinant DNA. Director's Report in the Annual Report of Cold Spring Harbor Laboratory.

Watson J.D. 1979. DNA folly continues. *New Republic* **180:** 12.

Watson J.D. 1979. The DNA biohazard canard. *Time Magazine,* January 31.

Watson J.D. 1979. Let us stop regulating DNA. *Nature* 278: 113.

Watson J.D. 1979. Academic thinkers and the real world. Director's Report in the Annual Report of Cold Spring Harbor Laboratory.

Watson J.D. 1980. Sixth Daniel C. Baker, Jr. Memorial Lecture. Induction of cancer by DNA viruses. *Ann. Otol. Rhinol. Laryngol.* **89:** 489–496.

Watson J.D. 1980. Maintaining high-quality cancer research in a zero-sum era. Director's Report in the Annual Report of Cold Spring Harbor Laboratory.

Watson J.D. and Tooze J. 1981. *The DNA story: A documentary history of gene cloning.* W.H. Freeman, San Francisco, California.

Watson, J.D. 1981. Striving for excellence. In *Excellence: The pursuit, the commitment, the achievement,* pp. 32–39. Corporate Affairs Department of LTV Corporation, Dallas, Texas.

Watson J.D. 1981. Cancer is a solvable problem. Director's Report in the Annual Report of Cold Spring Harbor Laboratory.

Watson J.D., Tooze J., and Kurtz D.T. 1982. *Recombinant DNA: A short course.* Scientific American Books, New York.

Baltimore D., Berg P., Bloch K.E., Brown D.D., Kornberg A., Nathans D., Smith H.O., Watson J.D., and Thomas L. 1982. Letter: Plea to the scientific community. *Science* **216:** 1046.

Watson J.D. 1982. Academic scientists become entrepreneurs. Director's Report in the Annual Report of Cold Spring Harbor Laboratory.

Alberts B., Bray D., Lewis J., Raff M. Roberts K., and Watson J.D., 1983. *Molecular biology of the cell.* Garland Publishing Inc., New York.

Watson J.D. 1983. Introduction: Double Helix 35th Anniversary Conference. *Nature* **302:** 651–652.

Watson J.D. 1984. Creating new life. *Omni,* May, vol. 6. Interview.

Watson J.D. 1984. Setting priorities for the future. Director's Report in the Annual Report of Cold Spring Harbor Laboratory.

Watson J.D. 1985. Moving on to human DNA. Director's Report in the Annual Report of Cold Spring Harbor Laboratory.

Watson J.D. 1986. From understanding to manipulating DNA. In *The positive sum strategy: Harnessing technology for economic growth* (ed. R. Landau and N. Rosenberg), pp. 213–225. National Academy Press, Washington, D.C.

Watson J.D. 1986. A Human Genome Project. Director's Report in the Annual Report of Cold Spring Harbor Laboratory.

Watson J.D. 1987. Minds that live for science. *New Scientist,* May 21, pp. 63–66.

Watson J.D. 1987. Honesty and decency in scientific research. Director's Report in the Annual Report of Cold Spring Harbor Laboratory.

Watson J.D. 1988. Working for the government—The Human Genome Project gets going. Director's Report in the Annual Report of Cold Spring Harbor Laboratory.

Watson J.D. 1989. The DNA gold rush (Jan.) *Research* **9:** 7.

Watson J.D. and Jordan E. 1989. The Human Genome Program at the National Institutes of Health. *Genomics* **5:** 654–656.

Watson J.D. 1989. A room with a view...For a few dollars more. *BIOtechnol. Education* **1:** 3–5.

Watson J.D. 1989. The science for beating down cancer. Director's Report in the Annual Report of Cold Spring Harbor Laboratory.

Watson J.D. 1990. The Human Genome Project: Past, present and future. *Science* **248:** 44–49.

Watson J.D. 1990. Bragg's foreword to *The double helix.* In *The legacy of Sir Lawrence Bragg* (ed. J.M. Thomas and Sir D. Phillips), pp. 111–113. The Royal Institution, London.

Watson J.D. 1990. First word. *Omni,* vol. 12, pp. 6–7.

Watson J.D. 1990. The Human Genome Project and international health. *J. Am. Med. Assoc.* **263:** 3322–3324.

Watson J.D. 1990. Letters to the editor: Genome Project maps path of diseases and drugs. *The New York Times,* Saturday, October 13.

Watson J.D. 1990. Looking ahead—The next one hundred years. Director's Report in the Annual Report of Cold Spring Harbor Laboratory.

Juengst E.T. and Watson J.D. 1991. Human genome research and the responsible use of new genetic knowledge. *J. Int. Bioethique* **2:** 99–102.

Watson J.D. 1991. Salvador E. Luria (1912–1991). *Nature* **350:** 113.

Watson J.D. 1991. Salvador E. Luria (13 August 1912–6 February 1991). *Proc. Am. Philos. Soc.* **143:** 681–683.

Watson J.D. 1991. Genes and the legacy of psychiatric illness. *The decade of the brain,* Spring, vol. 2, issue 2.

Watson J.D. 1991. The impact of the Human Genome Project. Beckman DU Symposium, April 10, Arnold and Mabel Beckman Center, Irvine, California.

Watson J.D. 1991. Too many noughts. *Nature* **350:** 550.

Watson J.D. 1991. The human genome initiative: A statement of need. *Hosp. Pract.* **26:** 69–73.

Watson J.D. 1991. In pursuit of the genetic grail. In *Chronika: A celebration of science* (ed. R.A. McCabe et al.), pp. 94–95. Athens College, Greece.

Watson J.D. 1991. Moving forward with the Human Genome Project. Director's Report in the Annual Report of Cold Spring Harbor Laboratory.

Watson J.D. and Cook-Deegan R.M. 1991. Origins of the Human Genome Project. *FASEB J.* **5:** 8 11.

Watson J.D. 1992. Tribute to the memory of Dr. Harry Eagle (1945–1992). *Einstein Q.* **10:** 66–67.

Watson J.D., Gilman M., Witkowski J.A., and Zoller M. 1992. *Recombinant DNA,* 2nd edition. Scientific American Books, New York.

Watson J.D. 1992. Early speculations and facts about RNA templates. In *The RNA world* (ed. R.F. Gesteland and J.F. Atkins), pp. xv–xxiii. Cold Spring Harbor Laboratory Press, Cold Spring Harbor, New York.

Watson J.D. 1992. Funding sources for research: Federal and corporate. Director's Report in the Annual Report of Cold Spring Harbor Laboratory.

Watson J.D. 1993. Why Britain's science cannot be sold short. *The Mail,* March 21.

Watson J.D. 1993. Initial implications of the double helix. Introductory issue, April 25. *Structure,* p. iii.

Watson J.D. 1993. Looking forward. *Gene* **135:** 309–315.

Watson J.D. 1993. Succeeding in science: Some rules of thumb. *Science* **261:** 1812–1813.

Watson J.D. 1993. Building our science, preserving our environment. Director's Report in the Annual Report of Cold Spring Harbor Laboratory.

Watson J.D. and Sher G.S. 1994. Does research in the former Soviet Union have a future? *Science* **264:** 1280–1281.

Watson J.D. 1994. Foreword. In *The polymerase chain reaction* (ed. K. Mullis et al.), pp. v–viii. Birkhäuser, Boston, Massachusetts.

Watson J.D. 1994. Toward a biological understanding of human nature. President's essay in the Annual Report of Cold Spring Harbor Laboratory.

Watson J.D. 1995. Values from a Chicago upbringing. In *DNA: The double helix—Perspective and prospective at forty years* (ed. D.A. Chambers). *Ann. N.Y. Acad. Sci.* **758:** 194–197.

Watson J.D. 1995. The Human Genome Project—Ten years later. President's essay in the Annual Report of Cold Spring Harbor Laboratory.

Watson J.D. 1996. Genes and politics. President's essay in the Annual Report of Cold Spring Harbor Laboratory.

Watson J.D. 1997. A laboratory for tough risk-takers. President's essay in the Annual Report of Cold Spring Harbor Laboratory.

Watson J.D. 1997. Genes and politics. *J. Mol. Med.* **75:** 624–636.

Watson J.D. 1997. Good gene, bad gene: What is the right way to fight the tragedy of genetic disease? *Time Magazine*, p. 86, Winter 1997–1998.

Watson J.D. 1998. Alfred D. Hershey: Hershey heaven. *The New York Times Magazine*, January 4.

Watson J.D. 1998. Afterword. Five days in Berlin. In *Murderous science. Elimination by scientific selection of Jews, Gypsies, and others in Germany, 1933–1945* (by B. Müller-Hill), Cold Spring Harbor Laboratory Press, Cold Spring Harbor, New York.

Watson J.D. 1998. Lessons for our new graduate school. President's essay in the Annual Report of Cold Spring Harbor Laboratory.

Watson J.D. 1999. All for the good: Why genetic engineering must soldier on. *Time Magazine* **153:** 91.

Watson J.D. 2000. *A passion for DNA: Genes, genomes, and society.* Cold Spring Harbor Laboratory Press, Cold Spring Harbor, New York.

Watson J.D. 2001. The human genome revealed. *Genome Res.* **11:** 1803–1804.

Watson J.D. 2001. Foreword. The human genome revealed, 2001. In *The human genome* (ed. C. Dennis and R. Gallagher). Palgrave Press, United Kingdom.

Gershon E.S., Kelsoe J.R., Kendler K.S., and Watson J.D. 2001. A scientific opportunity. *Science* **294:** 957.

Watson J.D. 2001. Rules for graduates. In *A passion for DNA: Genes, genomes, and society*, pp. 127–129. Cold Spring Harbor Laboratory Press, Cold Spring Harbor, New York. (U.S. paperback edition.)

Watson J.D. 2001. The pursuit of happiness. In *A passion for DNA: Genes, genomes, and society*, pp. 235–238. Cold Spring Harbor Laboratory Press, Cold Spring Harbor, New York. (U.S. paperback edition.)

Watson J.D. 2001. The human genome revealed. In *A passion for DNA: Genes, genomes, and society*, pp. 239–244. Cold Spring Harbor Laboratory Press, Cold Spring Harbor, New York. (U.S. paperback edition.)

Watson J.D. 2001. *Genes, girls and Gamow: After fhe double helix.* Oxford University Press, United Kingdom (also published by Knopf [2002] in the United States).

Watson J.D. with Berry A. 2003. *DNA: The secret of life.* Alfred A. Knopf, New York.

INDEX